NEVER A LOVE SONG

My Life as an Aspie's Wife

By

Asperger Wife

Website: Aspergerwife.com

Email: aspergerwife@yahoo.com

Copyright © 2011 by Asperger Wife. All rights reserved.

ISBN 978-1-105-32781-0

Library of Congress Cataloging-in-Publication Data

Wife, Asperger

Never a Love Song

ISBN 978-1-105-32781-0

   1.Wife, Asperger 2. Relationships 3. Asperger's 4. AS 5. Autism

First Edition December 2011

Cover Design by Asperger Wife

This book is lovingly dedicated
to all Asperger Wives

CONTENTS

INTRODUCTION

If you are reading this book, most likely you are acquainted with someone who has Asperger's Syndrome (AS) and/or are interested in finding out more about it. Perhaps someone you know may have it and you want to confirm your suspicions.

While I have including the basics about AS to help you in your search, my main goal is to just share my own personal story of what it is like actually living with a man with the disorder.

You won't read about any great psychological breakthroughs or find any new revelations and treatments for AS on these pages, so if that is your reason for picking up this book, you can stop here. You will read, however, about an NT/AS marriage as told by someone who lives it every single day. I have tried to be as candid and honest as possible, avoiding exaggerations, so as to enlighten others as to what such a relationship is like.

Had I know anything at all about Asperger's when I met my husband; it would have saved me years of self-doubt, many tears, and the physical problems resulting from suppressing feelings for so long. Thankfully, I finally find the truth as to why my husband behaved as he did. It was actually a relief for I finally had an answer—Asperger's Syndrome!

I want Asperger's Syndrome to be known world-wide and given just as much press and coverage as other diseases. Things are changing and the public is becoming more aware, but there's a long way to go before everybody knows exactly what AS is and what it involves.

Just as Christians feel the need to tell others how to gain heaven and avoid hell, my mission in writing this book is to share my experiences with AS, both good and bad, to warn others as to how difficult an NT/AS relationship can be. I also desire to help others discern if it really is AS that is causing someone they know or love to act a little "quirky" or "different" than what is considered normal. It is my hope they would encourage the person with AS to get the help they need so they can better manage their disorder.

If someone is thinking about entering into a serious dating or marriage relationship with an Aspie, they need to go in to it with their eyes wide open, knowing exactly what to expect and the problems that may lay ahead.

I know of no NT/AS relationship that runs smoothly and is a piece of cake, but many people that write me are so frustrated, hurt and disillusioned that they can't take it any more and end up divorced. Had they been informed early on that their mate had AS, they would most likely have altered their plans or at the least, learned how to cope by joining a support group for family members of those with Asperger's and Autism.

Unfortunately, many people only find out later in life that they or someone they know has Asperger's. Why is that? Because the public has not been made aware of its prevalence and its symptoms have not been discussed at length on television talk shows and in the press.

People may argue that revealing the negative aspects of a NeuroTypical/Asperger Syndrome relationship will do more harm than good. I beg to differ in that it will help people to enter such relationships knowing in advance what to expect, not stumbling in the dark for years, groping blindly for answers to some vague something that covers your life like a shroud, as was my experience.

It is not my intent to offend any Aspies who read this book, as I realize they have a desire to love and be loved like everyone else. I just find it difficult to maintain a balance to where I can help one group without offending another. My story is just that, "MY story." It is not sugar-coated to make it palatable for everyone, but it is an honest account of my own marriage. Many readers will see similarities in their own Aspie's behavior.

The names and locations have all been changed to protect our privacy and to not cause embarrassment to my husband or our family.

If you have comments or questions about anything you have read here, you may contact me through my website: www.aspergerwife.com.

Chapter One - Asperger's Syndrome - The Basics

Asperger syndrome (AS) is a developmental disorder--an autism spectrum disorder (ASD), one of a distinct group of neurological conditions characterized by a greater or lesser degree of impairment in language and communication skills, as well as repetitive or restrictive patterns of thought and behavior. Unlike children with autism, children with AS retain their early language skills.

The most distinguishing symptom of AS is a child's obsessive interest in one object or topic to the exclusion of any other. Children with AS want to learn everything about their topic of interest and their conversations with others will be about little else.

Their expertise, high level of vocabulary, and formal speech patterns make them seem like whiz kids.

Other characteristics of AS include repetitive routines or rituals; peculiarities in speech and language; socially and emotionally inappropriate behavior and the inability to interact successfully with peers; problems with non-verbal communication; and clumsy uncoordinated motor movements.

Children with AS are isolated because of their poor social skills and narrow interests. They may approach other people, but make normal conversation impossible by inappropriate or eccentric behavior, or by wanting only to talk about their one favorite topic of interest.

Children with AS usually have a history of developmental delays in motor skills such as pedaling a bike, catching a ball, or climbing outdoor play equipment. They are often awkward and poorly coordinated with a walk that can appear either stilted or bouncy. Many children with AS are often bullied by their peers.

General Characteristics of Aspies

Person's with AS usually:

- May be visual thinkers and learners.
- Are very literal in their thoughts and interpretations
- Have average to above average IQ's
- May have strong verbal skills

- Are routine oriented and rule-based in their behavior
- Are not flexible in their thinking
- May have difficulty socializing with others
- Obsess around their favorite things and interests
- Have difficulty understanding another's point of view and ideas
- Have difficulty reading the behavior of others
- Experience difficulty in making or keeping eye contact
- Are uncoordinated and dislike physical activity including sports
- Are very vulnerable to stress and high levels of anxiety
- Find emotions difficult to express, discuss, or understand
- Have sensory integration difficulties and seek sensory stimulation and input

Person's with AS may display some or all of the following characteristics:

- Socially awkward
- Naive and gullible (easy target for bullies)
- Often unaware of others' feelings
- Limited play and leisure skills
- Unusually accurate memory for details
- Difficulty with sleeping or eating
- Trouble with organizational skills
- Easily upset by changes in routines
- Unusual and very intense areas of interests
- Lack peer and friendship establishment
- Limited or immature conversation skills (difficulties with give and take)
- Unusual or conflicting body language or facial expressions, e.g., smiling when telling something sad
- Unusual speech patterns (repetitive and/or irrelevant remarks)
- Unusually loud, high or monotone voice or stilted manner of speaking
- Difficulty managing stress, frustration

Did you know?

Actress Daryl Hannah was "blacklisted" from Hollywood because she suffered from Asperger's Syndrome. She was diagnosed with AS early in her career and admits it almost ruined her professional life because she was so nervous of doing promotions as it involved talking to lots of people. She never went on talk shows, never went to premieres and going to the Academy Awards were painful for her that she'd almost faint just walking down the red carpet. She was so socially awkward and uncomfortable that it led to her eventually getting blacklisted.

According to estimates from the National Institutes of Health, two out of 10,000 children have AS, which sits on the autism spectrum of disorders. However, Asperger's Syndrome wasn't widely known until the 1980s.

While there's no cure for the disease, effective therapeutic treatments have emerged to help patients with Asperger's maintain independent lives.

There's an 80% unemployment rate for those with AS because of the challenges with social skills and sensory issues.

The divorce rate among those in NT/AS relationships is estimated to be as high as 87%.

Typically, those with AS, are at a loss regarding the language of love and the emotions involved with it, most of which is nonverbal. They will have difficulty recognizing and using it.

Some famous people suspected of having Asperger's are: Abraham Lincoln, Michael Jackson, Emily Dickinson, Mozart, Beethoven, George Washington, Bill Gates, John Denver, Albert Einstein, Jim Henson, and Steven Spielberg.

Chapter Two - How We Met

Single for a few years after the end of my second marriage, I was persuaded by friends to go out with them and do something fun. They said I needed a life besides work and caring for my aged mother. At their constant urging, I finally gave in and joined them at a place ten miles away where bikers hung out on the bar side of the saloon, and line dancing took place on the other. We had a blast as I love to dance and it was great exercise.

Soon line dancing became a regular part of my life. I particularly liked the fact that I could go alone if my friends weren't available, and that I could dance without a partner. I'm a tall, long-legged woman and it's hard to find a dance partner tall enough to twirl me around the floor.

At that time, I had decided I'd remain single at least until my mother passed away, and vowed to <u>never</u> date a man I'd met in a bar. My two previous husbands were both alcoholics and I'd had enough of that type of personality to last a lifetime.

One Friday night my friends and I drove to a crowded dance hall in another town, and that is where I was formally introduced to Steve. He was quiet, rather shy, and didn't say much, but when the music started, he'd be one of the first on the dance floor. He was a couple of inches shorter than me, but in his cowboy boots, we were about the same height. He was skinny and ruggedly handsome, and looked good in a pair of jeans and cowboy hat.

Over the course of several weeks, I had a chance to observe Steve in various situations. What impressed me most was that he didn't feel the need to talk a whole lot and that he seemed trustworthy. It bothered me when I'd see guys boasting of their conquests and bringing different women to the bar on separate nights. Steve wasn't like that, but seemed like a genuinely nice guy.

During line dance lessons, the instructor kept pairing Steve and me up for the couples dances, which allowed us to get better acquainted.

Another friend at the usual hangout was actually the main one responsible for getting Steve and I together. I told her in confidence that I was slightly attracted to Steve, and she and her boyfriend set up a double date for us. After that one date, we soon became fast friends and were going to country concerts and other places together. We were inseparable at that time.

I didn't think much about it at the time, but Steve and I never had really deep discussions. We mainly talked about where we were going next and when he'd be around to pick me up.

Early on, however, I was impressed with Steve's uncanny ability to recall names, dates, and events. His outstanding memory won us tickets once to see Wynonna Judd in concert when we won a trivia contest for he knew the answer to the tough question posed by the emcee.

Steve, though young, has older ideas, possibly from spending so much time with his parents and their friends. Living at home well into his thirties also had to be another reason for his interacting well with those older than him. Maybe that was part of the attraction he had for me, at least initially. Another reason was most likely because I was nice to him.

Our political views were also in sync and we always seemed to get along well together. I can't recall our ever raising our voices in an argument in all the time we went together. Steve was a quiet, mellow guy who never showed anger or other emotions, for that matter.

After about five or six weeks of dating, on a cold, wintry night outside of yet another line dance establishment, Steve told me he loved me.

Looking back, I wonder if he didn't say it only because he thought the timing was right as it seemed he was following instructions in some book. He often seemed quite mechanical in his actions.

I'm not sure that Steve really "felt" love for me, as I'm not sure if he's capable of feeling in the way a normal person would. Emotions just never seemed to affect Steve. He's pretty much always the same plain vanilla kind of guy when it comes to his behavior. In a way it was comforting as the men in my previous relationships were quite volatile and it was frightening to always have to be on guard, not knowing if they were going to hurt me physically or not. I was confident that would never be an issue with Steve.

Steve always doubts his abilities and I set out to build him up and encourage him by telling him he could "rope the moon" or do anything he dreamed of doing. That was before I realized that Steve only does what Steve wants, when he wants to do it, and that he's afraid to step out and try new things. When he has, he quickly loses interest, and seems to have a self-defeatist attitude. He blames his failure on many things, but the real one, which is that he's afraid to succeed.

I attribute Steve's lack of confidence to his mother who would give him instructions, then change them midstream. She was never satisfied and quite hard to please. She'd send Steve to the store with a list of things to get and when he'd return, she'd find something wrong with what he bought and have him return most of them. At Christmas, she'd tell everyone what she wanted and then have them take the gifts back to the store and get a refund.

When Steve would go out to a restaurant with his father and mother, his mother would be so picky and complaining that it was embarrassing. She'd find fault with everything from the food to the service. One restaurant told them they were no longer welcome there and banned them from ever returning.

Steve's sister had to see a psychiatrist for a time because of being raised by such a mother. It about drove her crazy. No wonder Steve had little confidence and needed someone to tell him exactly what to do. That is what his mother did to him for his entire life. He was ordered around and told what to think, what to do, and when to do it. He was not allowed to think for himself.

Learning about Steve's history, of course I felt sorry for him and jumped in to caregiver mode. I wanted to make his life easier, build up his self-esteem and help him forget about his difficult home life. That was probably another reason for our getting on together so well. We both were never validated by our families and were never taken seriously. Our opinions never mattered and didn't count. It may have been on a subconscious level, but it was enough to attract us to one another.

Chapter Three - In the Beginning

Steve was several years younger than me, but since our relationship was more than friends, less than lovers, the age difference didn't matter. We enjoyed being together as we got along very well. That is, until his mother began to cause problems and complicate things.

Steve had only one previous relationship--ever! It had ended seven years before we met when his family ran the girl off because they didn't like her. I doubt if anyone would have been good enough for Steve in their eyes as they exerted too much control over him and manipulated him easily. He still lived at home, never having been married, even though he was in his mid-thirties.

After several weeks, we mutually decided to break off our relationship. It hurt a great deal because I really liked Steve. He wanted to continue to be friends, but he was obsessed with another girl who had already told him there was no future for them together. I stated that I cared too much for him and thought it best to end things since he was chasing after someone else. The girl was dating another guy, but Steve still obsessed about her and hoped she would eventually be his.

I didn't care to be in a love triangle, so I intended to make it a clean break. We were in my car in the parking lot of the place where we danced many dances together when I shook his hand and said goodbye. He said he wanted to kiss me goodbye, but I refused. It wasn't easy, but I knew I had to let go and move on.

I cried that entire night, mostly because I again felt rejected and unloved. It was like a repeat of my past relationships. I went dancing with friends to various other places and tried not to care that Steve was out of the picture, but I did. It wasn't so much that I loved Steve, but that I felt worthless because of yet another rejection in my life.

Due to past experiences and low self-esteem, I allowed myself to be attracted to men who, though often quite charming, treated me poorly. I guess that is why I had strong feelings for Steve and tolerated rudeness by his mother, as well as by him, longer than I should have. It was abuse to which I had become accustomed, so, sick as it was, I put up with it.

If I was stronger at the time, when Steve would laugh and think it funny that his mother would hang up on me whenever I'd call him, I would have told him to take a hike right then and there. Instead, I did nothing to change the situation, and Steve never did confront his mother about her rude behavior.

A couple of weeks after our breakup when I had finally gotten myself together, Steve called, quickly asking me to not hang up. He apologized and begged for another chance. He said he was confused and didn't know what he wanted when we broke up. He seemed sincere, so in a vulnerable moment, I said "okay" and we soon picked up where we left off.

Chapter Four – Peculiarities

What You Don't Know CAN Hurt You

One thing that I noticed early on in our relationship was that Steve would never bring me flowers, candy, or little gifts to show he cared. Men I'd dated always bought me little gifts while "wooing" me. Not necessarily expensive things, but a single rose, or chocolates--something just to say, "You're special."

Evidently Steve's mother told him that if he took me out to dinner, I should be the one to leave the tip. Old-fashioned woman that I am, I felt that if he asked me out to a restaurant, then he should pick up the entire bill. I'd pay the tip, but drew the line when he's telling me how much to leave on the table.

With Steve and I going out every weekend, I told him that I preferred to eat at fast food places occasionally instead of always at a fancier restaurant. I was thinking of his budget and tried to make it easier for him. He wouldn't listen. He had to eat at a place where it was more expensive no matter what I preferred. To this day, Steve will ask where I want to eat and it really doesn't matter, because we always end up going to where Steve wants or getting take-out from wherever it is he wants. He will not change his routine.

On more than one occasion, we'd be driving down the road, and Steve would slowly pull his pickup truck to the side of the road. He'd reach in the back for something, and I smiled to myself, thinking he might be reaching for a little token of affection with which to surprise me, but instead, he'd reach for his jacket or something else. No little gift ever materialized.

Our birthdays are a week apart and the gifts I'd buy him would lay unopened or unused for months afterwards, even though I selected them with great care. I'd take it personally and thought he could at least act like he enjoyed what I'd given him. He had the same, nonchalant attitude about everything.

One gift I bought after we'd been going out for over eight months was having us both have our photos done professionally at a local photography studio. Steve kept procrastinating about getting it done and kept making excuses, saying he *needed to do that*, his most-used phrase. Finally, in frustration, I told him to just go there by himself before the gift certificate expired, which he promptly did.

Steve is very self-centered and clueless about a lot of things. He seemed incapable of comprehending my feelings and that the intent was to have a nice photo of us together. To this day, he rarely takes a photo of me unless I specifically ask him to, which isn't often. He never even carried a photo of me in his wallet until I mentioned it to him that guys usually carry a picture of their girlfriend to show their buddies.

Steve drove an old, beat-up pickup truck and to look at it, filled with trash, you'd think he lived in the poorest part of town. When we went on our first real date which was with another couple, I picked up the whole check for everyone, because I thought he was too poor to afford it and didn't want to embarrass him. I later found he lived in one of the wealthiest subdivisions in town and came from an affluent family.

One of the odd things I noticed about Steve when I first met him was his stiff, stilted movements when he walked, and the nasal tone to his voice. He also had a very weird laugh (like the girl in the movie, *Mozart & the Whale*).

When I'd try to have a conversation with him, he was not focusing on what I was saying. He'd get a weird smile on his face and look away. For a long time, I thought he was just trying to stifle laughing about something he thought funny about me. Instead, he was thinking of something not even remotely connected to what I was saying. He would do that every time I tried to talk to him. It was quite frustrating to even try to have a meaningful conversation with him.

Steve would never be one to tell you if you had spinach in your teeth or if you were dragging toilet paper on your shoe. He'd let you be embarrassed when you'd walk into a crowd of people with the back of your dress stuck inside your pantyhose. I tried to get the point across that when a person is dating someone, they should mention it if they see something that could cause embarrassment to the other, when the other person can't see it themselves. It was polite and considerate to do such a thing. I'm not sure if I got through to him or not. Steve rarely listens or cares what it is I have to say.

When Steve and I would go out, he'd pick me up in his old, beat-up truck and never clear the front seat of tapes, papers, receipts, etc. before I got there. I'd have to rearrange the debris in order to sit down.

His driving left a lot to be desired, as well. Aspies can only focus on one thing at a time, it appears, and when Steve and I were together, he'd weave all over the road like a drunk driver. It would scare me to death! One time we were pulled over by a country cop who saw the out-of-state license plate and told Steve he was weaving. He let him go with the comment that he was probably just not used to driving curvy country roads. If he only knew that Steve drives that way on straight roads, too.

When Steve goes to park his truck, it is also frightening. He does not slow down until he's in the spot and will always come within inches of hitting another vehicle. His perception of how close he is has been amazingly accurate, but it still produces anxiety. He also has to park in between two cars, even if there are single spaces closer to the entrance of the store. He must park between two cars or close to at least one or he's not satisfied.

Steve worked at the same job for six years and had not had one raise in all that time. He was reliable and a hard worker so it was hard for me to understand why he stayed there without an increase in pay. When I first observed him in action in the workplace, I finally understood. He was so disorganized that his work area looked like a tornado had hit. It would take him ten times longer to finish a task than it would anyone else, because of his lack of organizational skills. The end result was perfect, but getting to that point was incomprehensible to an observer. He seemed to lack common sense when it came to doing projects that required a plan.

At my urging, Steve finally got a better job a few years later and has a decent salary and health benefits. I thank God for watching over him and keeping him steadily employed as many people with AS find it hard to keep jobs due to their limitations.

Life is not a matter of having good cards,
but of playing a poor hand well. --Robert Louis Stevenson

Chapter Five – The Object of my Affection

One thing I learned early on in our relationship was that Steve did not have one ounce of romance within him. I longed for something, anything to add romance to our relationship. I even bought him a book to help him out, since he hadn't dated much before we met. The book was "100 Ways to be Romantic." He never even opened it. I dropped hints, I told him flat out, yet he never followed through on anything in the least that would be romantic.

I am a very sentimental woman who is a true romantic at heart. I am the type that presses flowers into books so I can remember happy times. I write in journals to capture special moments on paper. I thrive on romance. With Steve, I never had so much as a candy wrapper to put in a memory book. He didn't see the need, even though it was something that would make me happy.

As an amateur singer/songwriter, I even wrote and recorded a song about our dating relationship. Little did I know that it was just describing typical Asperger's behavior. Also, at that time, I had never even heard of Asperger's.

I've written books and had them published, but Steve has not read one of them. He only reads what is of interest to him.

Immediately after Steve and I began dating, he picked out a song as "our song." It had all the appearances of a romantic gesture, but his choice left me having self-doubts. He chose the song "When You Say Nothing at All" by Alison Krauss. On the surface, it seemed okay, I guess, but I silently wondered if he was trying to tell me I talked too much. I have one of those bubbly, talkative personalities so I thought he was maybe trying to tell me to shut up.

It wasn't about me, I later realized, but about himself. He has never been much of a talker and was trying to tell me he wanted to be accepted in spite of his lack of conversational skills.

I recall being at his sister's house on special occasions, and would observe Steve as he would set himself down at the table right in the midst of everyone as they bantered back and forth. He, himself, would not utter a single word. His dad would often comment about his being so quiet.

Unlike most Aspies, Steve does like social events as long as it's with people he knows otherwise it makes him anxious and more awkward in his actions. He seems to enjoy listening to everyone talking, soaking it all in, with only a rare comment of his own.

On our first *Sweetest Day* after we'd been dating a year, Steve's dad had him working on a house he owned late into the evening. His dad wouldn't let him leave to keep our preplanned date, and Steve didn't tell him that we had dinner plans.

I was so upset, but instead of understanding my anger, Steve repeated to me what his dad told him, "It's just another Hallmark holiday to make you spend money." I told Steve that might be true, but when you love someone, you should consider it another opportunity to show how much you care. He said, "Well, yeah..." and then just blew it off, as always; again, no romance, whatsoever.

A part of me always felt sad when I thought about it, but I cared for Steve, so I set my feelings aside. It was something I had to do more and more often as time went by.

Yet it still doesn't stop me from wishing there was romance in my marriage, for it is what I miss the most.

I can complain because rose bushes have thorns,
or rejoice because thorn bushes have roses.
It's all how you look at it. -- J. Kenfield Morley

Chapter Six – The Wedding

In my life while holding down a job as well as caring for my elderly mother, things were rapidly changing. I ended up moving out of state, but Steve and I kept in touch through e-mails and by phone.

After a few months of a long distance relationship, we began thinking that maybe we should get married. So, on an overcast day thick with heavy, dark clouds, Steve proposed in a grand way (only because I suggested the method myself).

I had told Steve when I believed that we would always be just friends that I would only marry again if the man loved me enough to write in the sky that he loved me. Well, Steve did the next best thing. He hired a plane with a banner that read "AW, I love you, will you marry me?"

I smile and wonder how many other men took advantage of that same proposal as the plane kept circling and flying around for a half an hour or so over a heavily populated area.

Steve's dad said it was a waste of money, but I felt it was a good investment as it sealed the deal in my mind that Steve and I were meant to be together. I said "yes."

After the proposal, we waited several months to tie the knot because I didn't want to rush into marriage again. After two failed marriages, I was so unsure and extremely anxious as to whether or not I was making the right decision. I talked with a counselor, trying to make up my mind, and even to the very night we were wed, I was still so very uncertain whether or not I'd done the right thing.

Even though Steve's mother had passed away by that time, I knew his family would continue to cause grief and I wasn't sure I wanted to deal with that, as well as other problems that I knew were forthcoming. I should have listened to my instincts.

I wanted a small intimate wedding. Steve initially agreed, but wanted his entire family present which would make for a larger gathering and would defeat the purpose. I tried to honor his wishes and to also please his dad and sister, putting my desires aside. Resigned to the fact it was not going to be my dream wedding, the only thing I asked was that I get to dance with my husband that night.

We spent a small fortune on a type of wedding that I didn't want. It was much larger than intended, and ended up to be a near disaster because at the last minute, his family refused to help with the work involved, as promised.

Two days before the wedding, Steve's sister called and began yelling at me on the phone. She was deliberately stirring up trouble and supposedly was speaking for her dad, who was opposed to our getting married. I asked if she was trying to run me off as she did his previous girlfriend, and told her that, if so, it wasn't going to work.

That was the first time (and the last) that normally mild-mannered Steve actually stood up to his sister and his dad. He firmly stated that if they had any objections, they could just stay away from the wedding. He wanted them there, of course, and was filled with anxiety over the situation.

We didn't know until the actual evening of our wedding whether or not they would even attend. They did show up, but his dad had such a sad face throughout the evening, you could tell he wasn't happy at all about this union since I had been married before. Ironically, his sister had been married before, too, but when you're judging someone, you don't consider that you have the same faults. Since that time, his sister's second marriage failed and her relationship with a live-in boyfriend just ended.

Steve's dad a year later began living with another woman with whom he had been acquainted with for years. They had met at a previous workplace and we suspect they were "involved" even while Steve's mother was alive as we have proof in the form of photographs.

When they wed, they did it in a surprise court house ceremony with NONE of the family present. We found out about it some time later when they expected us to come to a restaurant to celebrate after the fact. It still bothers me that they had the type of small, intimate wedding they wanted, and yet Steve and I sacrificed our own dream wedding to honor their wishes.

Steve and I wed on a Saturday evening in early September. A relative who is a minister officiated.

An hour before the wedding I was still decorating the hall, along with my daughter and best friend. Steve's family didn't do anything to help, which made it very difficult for us. The lady in charge of the hall saw me working and said I'd better leave and go home and get ready for the wedding. I worked up until almost the last minute.

It was apparent that Steve's sister and her daughter, who always want to be the center of attention, were upset because they weren't asked to be in the wedding. Steve's niece sat with her arms folded and pouted all night long. My daughter was my maid of honor and Steve's best friend was the best man. My son wasn't in the wedding, either, but he didn't complain.

Though she never did apologize, Steve's sister tried to be friendly and took pictures of us after the wedding, most likely because she felt guilty about her behavior two nights previously. Unfortunately, because of her taking so many photographs, it caused a long delay in our even sitting down to dinner. The guests always wait for the bride and groom to eat first, so I know people had to be upset having to wait so long to dine.

If it wasn't for two dear friends and my daughter, the wedding would have been even worse. Besides helping to decorate the hall, they stayed to help clean up afterwards.

We had the hall rented for four hours, which should have been plenty of time, but the delay Steve's sister caused had the hall manager shooing us out the door as fast as she could. In my lace wedding dress, I cleared tables and packed up the huge amounts of uneaten food we had ordered. Many people got tired of waiting to eat and left, leaving us with an abundance of food. So much money wasted, but I did give away as much of the food as I could if I knew someone would really use it.

I only danced one brief dance with my husband, but the acoustics in the hall we rented were so bad, you could barely hear the music on the dance floor. I pasted a smile on my face the entire evening for the benefit of the guests, but my heart was so very heavy. I couldn't wait for the evening to end.

When I think back about it not being the wedding of my dreams, I am filled with deep regret. Every wedding anniversary causes me to relive the hurt. I didn't want to be reminded of how painful the memory of what should have been our most special day was, so I destroyed our wedding video. It didn't matter to Steve, because he would never have watched it anyway. We were married and that was enough for him.

Steve knew our wedding ceremony was not the one I had wanted, but he has never once offered to make it up to me or fulfill my desire of celebrating an anniversary by simply going out and dancing slow dances together in each other's arms. He's incapable of comprehending just how much it would have meant to me to have one romantic encounter to replace the bad memory of our wedding whenever our anniversary rolls around.

Every year, if we celebrate at all, we do it with take-out food or by going out to eat at a restaurant of Steve's choosing. When I tell him what I'd really like to do, he just stares with that Aspie stare I've come to know so well, and, as usual, says, "I need to do that..."

On our ninth anniversary, Steve and I stopped celebrating our anniversary. No card. No gift. No special dinner. We just wished each other a happy anniversary and left it at that. It was the same on our tenth anniversary.

We both know that our marriage is pretty much dead or dying, but out of habit we won't cut the marital cord. I'm not sure of what Steve's reasons are for sticking around exactly, but I feel it has more to do with his comfortable routine of me being there meeting his housekeeping needs than anything else. If he still loves me, he does little to show it.

Chapter Seven - An Asperger's Marriage

After a brief honeymoon, Steve and I quickly settled in to married life and moved into his house. He had moved out of his parents' home at the age of 38--finally, while we were dating and with my urging. I owned a house in another state, but sold it a few years after we were married. We didn't move into it because of Steve's job.

Our line dancing days were long gone, and married life kicked in. Due to the severity of traumas I experienced within a very short time before we were married, I was placed on disability and unable to work, but received a Social Security check each month. We fell into a pattern where I basically paid for my own needs, and Steve paid for his.

Every morning I would rise early (before 5:00 a.m.) with Steve to make his breakfast, pack his lunch and see him off to work. He never asked me to, but I cared about him and wanted to be a good wife.

I'd often include little love notes inside his lunch bag. Not once did he ever comment or mention them. Gradually, I just stopped writing them, because of his lack of response. It was another cup of water thrown on the spark of romance by Steve.

When Steve returns home from work each day, I always ask how his day went, and he always has the same answer. "Busy!" I'd try rephrasing the question, but he still won't elaborate. Always replies..."busy!"

Steve gave his heart to Jesus while we were still dating and we began attending church together regularly.   After we were married, we got into a routine that includes praying over our meals together at the kitchen counter and then he retreats to his den and closes the door. He eats in front of the computer and I eat in front of the television in our family room. I can honestly say that in all of the time we've been married we have only eaten one or two meals at our dining room table together. Steve prefers to be alone after working all day, and I try to not let it bother me.

It seems that Steve is always shutting me out in one way or another. He enters the bathroom and closes the door. He enters the bedroom, and closes the door. In any room he enters, the door always must be closed after him to shut me and our pets out.

I can often hear him muttering on the other side of the door and you'd think he was talking on the phone to someone, but in reality, he is having regular conversations with himself. He reminds me of those shaggy appearing, street people you'd see on park benches that do the same. I can't believe I'd married one!

I can recall that I often used the term rigid in referring to Steve. He was so set in his ways, seemingly more so, as time went on. He had a certain routine and if it was disrupted in any way, he would get upset with himself and begin throwing or breaking things. Behind closed doors, of course, rarely in front of me. He kept things bottled up inside, chewed his fingernails half way down the nail, and always appeared to have a very anxious disposition.

Steve never took his anger out on me, but always on himself or inanimate objects when things got too stressful at work. He kept things inside and only on rare occasions would he tell me bits and pieces of what was really bothering him. I guess when he was living at home for all those years; his family never validated him or his opinion. What he thought never mattered. He just silently complied with his family's wishes in whatever they asked him to do, so he learned to hold in his feelings.

A friend of Steve's since childhood told me that Steve's family used him and treated him like a servant. They'd have him cleaning, vacuuming, and ran him ragged. His mother more than once sent him out on the coldest of snowy nights to drive miles in search of one Charleston Chew candy bar. They'd have him laboring on different things often until 10:30 at night and he wouldn't be allowed to eat dinner until they were done. Consequently, Steve was a thin man with weird eating habits when we met. I changed all that and he soon gained weight with the regular meals I prepared for him.

One thing that I thought odd was that Steve, who has always been very polite, would ask if he could have a certain food or drink from the refrigerator, or if he could borrow a drill or something of mine. This was after we were married and I made it clear that what was mine was his and he could just take what he needed. He still does ask, but I gave up mentioning it to him. When he does ask, it makes me feel like he's a child asking his mother for a cookie and that he'd get in trouble if he just took one.

For three years, Steve tried hard to mask his little quirks and be a good husband, but as he settled into marriage and knew I was there for the long haul, he stopped trying to hide them. He just let his personality take over and pretty much did what made him comfortable. The behavior he had attempted to mask for so long was being revealed little by little as the weeks went by.

He used more soap and toilet paper than I ever knew one man could. What TP he uses each week would be the normal amount for a family of six. I'd ask him to conserve, but he'd look at me with what I refer to as that Aspie stare and never would even try, so the amount we spend on TP, napkins and paper towels has been ridiculous.

Our sink is constantly filled with dishes, because Steve cannot remember, though I remind him often, that once rinsed, they should be placed in the dishwasher.

Until I found out about AS, I always thought Steve was just lazy and that was why he was such a procrastinator and why he found it hard to start, let alone complete, projects around the house. He just finds it difficult to do anything outside of his normal routine. When he does, he gets filled with anxiety, so he keeps postponing tackling anything new.

Steve definitely showed obsessive/compulsive behavior traits, and I used to joke with him about it, not realizing at the time how serious the matter was.

For example, he cannot just cut the grass and leave the clippings fall on the lawn. He always has to bag the grass, even though what I've read from lawn care experts says that the grass seed should be left on the lawn every so often to make the grass healthier. I kept the article for Steve, but he didn't believe it. He continues to bag grass cuttings.

Steve is a big procrastinator and leaves tasks for years before he will attempt to finish them. We once were without electricity in our hall and bathroom, because Steve wouldn't take time to check out why the circuit breaker kept clicking off. Nine months later, I asked Steve's dad if he could motivate Steve to fix the problem. His dad came over after stating that Steve needed a good kick in the pants to get him going. The problem was found and fixed in just a couple of minutes. If Steve would have bothered to check out the problem himself nine months earlier, he would have found a wire had loosened and was causing a short in the bathroom outlet.

Another time during a very hot summer, our cat and I suffered from the effects of being without air-conditioning because Steve wouldn't check out why it wasn't working. In the fall, when he finally decided to do something about it, he found that the circuit breaker switch had clicked off and all he needed to do was to reset it. If I ever wanted to smack the man, it was then. He had told me he had checked the circuit breaker as one of the first things when it first stopped working so that's why I didn't check it myself.

In another chapter of this book, I have included a long list of Steve's peculiarities, which line up with typical Asperger's behavior. I know people with AS can be different as night and day, but there are many traits that are common to all Aspies. You may see some similarities between Steve and the Aspie in your life.

The pure, the beautiful, the bright, That stirred our hearts in youth, The impulse to a wordless prayer, The dreams of love and truth, The longings after something lost, The spirit's yearning cry, The strivings after better hopes, These things can never die.
—Sarah Doudney

Chapter Eight - Same House, Separate Lives

We were married three years when I had major exploratory surgery after a cancer scare. Feeling unlovely and badly in need of emotional support, Steve decided just three short months after my surgery that my snoring was so loud, it disrupted his sleep. This is very embarrassing for me to admit that I do snore, but Steve snores, too, but that didn't matter.

With my body scarred and the future uncertain as the doctors gave me a possible death sentence, Steve was not there for me emotionally. Thankfully, I had God to lean on and it was He Who helped me through the many dark, lonely days and nights when Steve would not reach out to help.

Feeling extremely hurt and dejected, I moved out of our bed and began sleeping in another bedroom. I cried many nights, because again I felt alone and rejected. He didn't even care or comprehend what I was going through and lacked the ability to understand my feelings or empathize with me.

Right before that, because we both had back problems, we had purchased a new, firm mattress set, but I only slept on it with him a couple of weeks. Steve, never a skilled lover in the first place, and never caring much for intimacy anyway, has not ever asked me to return to the master bedroom. When I'd bring up the subject, he'd say, "I need to do that," but never did. It was obvious that he preferred to sleep alone.

If I had one word to describe my life with Steve, it would be "lonely." I have felt isolated and alone throughout our marriage, but with two failed marriages behind me, I am determined to stick it out and continue to make this one work. I know Steve would never leave me, because he's grown comfortable with my being his housekeeper, cook and companion. He needs me for those reasons.

In reality, I am not a wife, but a roommate and a maid. We have become people who occupy the same house, but who go our separate ways. He does what he wants, and I do the same. We only come together to pray over our meals before heading to our own little corners of the house each evening.

During those early years of our marriage, I was filled with insecurities and self-doubt and Steve's behavior didn't help matters any. I had gone through a second painful divorce a few years before Steve and I met, and had just ended a long-distance relationship with another man who had bruised my already fragile ego. Why I allowed men who had problems of their own determine my self-worth, I will never know.

Looking back, I realize that for years I was reacting to Steve as if he were a "normal" person. Had I known he suffered from Asperger's Syndrome, it would have saved me much heartache and loads of tears. I kept thinking it was something in me that made me so worthless and unlovable, and that was why he kept pushing me away. I was so very wrong.

Nothing I could have done would have changed the situation. We still sleep in separate rooms in separate beds because Steve could never adjust to sleeping with someone else in the bed. It also interfered with the conversations he has with himself in the bedroom behind closed doors.

Chapter 9 – Behind Closed Doors

My friends think that my marriage is bliss and would be surprised to know what it's like behind closed doors. When Steve and I got engaged, however, every one of my friends was shocked and weren't afraid to admit it. We were the classic "odd couple." It wasn't just the difference in our ages, but in our personalities and outward appearances.

Steve was rather awkward and shy and I was more outgoing and socially adept. They knew we were good friends, but had no idea it would ever turn into marriage. I know they feared it wouldn't last with so many differences.

To prove them wrong, I've learned to maintain an outward appearance that all is well. So...I guess I can be considered a great pretender as a popular song from the sixties so aptly describes.

We went on two vacations two years apart early in our marriage, but Steve picked the locations. In fact, he never even considered that I might want to go someplace different. My opinion didn't (and doesn't) matter to him. Thankfully, the places he did pick were nice and we enjoyed the trips, but he already is working on the next places **he'd** like to visit without me.

As I write this, he is preparing to leave for a week to go camping by himself. It is how he is spending our vacation. We should be together, but I'll be home alone, as usual, taking care of our pets and the house.

We have a ritual that is repeated every week when it comes time to buying take-out food. The outcome is always the same; we do what Steve wants. He'll begin the conversation with asking me what I'd like to eat and from where. I'll mention a place, but if he doesn't feel in the mood for food from that restaurant, we'll get it from the place he wants.

I always give in and let him choose to prevent his pouting like a child. He rarely compromises and is used to getting his own way. I thought he was just spoiled, but it could be due to his AS. I can never be sure which one it is, so I try to not get upset and continue to let him do what he wants. I'm probably an enabler, but I've yet to discern when it's AS or when it's his own stubborn personality.

Steve gets obsessed easily with things he loves, and plunges headlong into whatever it is. He spends hours on end focusing on those things. One of them, for example, is Karen Carpenter. She's been dead for decades, but he has her cds, cassettes, photos, and listens to her music until it can make a normal person nauseous.

His computer is filled with information about her. He spends more time with her memory than he does me, his wife. He has had the same obsession at various times with John Denver, favorite old TV shows, and two or three favorite hobbies.

Steve also obsesses over any woman who is nice to him. I used to get jealous, but stopped doing that as I know he'd never cheat unless the other woman was the aggressor. Steve would not be considered a "catch" in today's world. He lacks social skills and is incapable of knowing how to give a woman what she wants.

In a relationship where one person has Asperger's, there is no give and take, it's all about the Aspie. They cannot seem to understand the needs of their partner, and only focus on what makes their life comfortable. They have their daily rituals and procrastinate when it comes to doing anything at all outside their normal routine.

Steve mainly takes care of himself and his needs. If the dog needs to be let out in the morning, I am the one to do it. He won't even stop to walk to the door to open it. He cannot have his routine disrupted, or else he gets anxious. I can count on one hand the number of times he has actually fed our two pets. He loves them, but can only realistically care for himself. He doesn't concern himself with their needing to be watered and fed.

As a child Steve banged his head against the fireplace when he got mad, and was often bullied by his peers because of his shyness and puny stature. He was unable to get a degree at junior college, although he attended three years. He said he didn't do well in school.

I didn't realize that those with AS can have self hatred, too, or try to harm themselves. I knew that Steve had serious problems when I found several of his work shirts with holes cut in them at the bottom of his closet. When I asked about them, he just ignored me and gave no answer.

The week before that, he had cut himself with a knife accidentally; at least that's what he said. He told me he was playing with it and it slipped. I'm not so sure. He said he almost asked me to take him to the hospital to get stitches it was bleeding so much.

Steve has a certain blank Aspie look that he uses whenever I ask about things he doesn't want to talk about. It is frustrating to see it for I know what's coming. He ignores me. Absolutely nothing makes me madder than when he walks away while I'm talking to him, which he does often. It can make my blood boil when he does this.

I must remember that he can only focus on one thing at a time, and that one thing demands ALL his attention or he gets anxious. If he's in the middle of doing something and I ask him a question, he often can't handle it, so he just leaves the room. It appears rude and it is, but Steve really can't seem to help it. It's just one way of dealing with things when he is overwhelmed or overly stressed.

After observing Steve's behavior for years, I knew he was not exactly what a person would call "normal," but I wasn't able to exactly put my finger on what you would call it. He was a contradiction--a mystery man. At times he showed high intelligence and was a veritable encyclopedia of knowledge, yet couldn't put together a simple project without making it a major undertaking akin to building a house.

He seemed to lack common sense and sometimes appeared like an imbecile. His way of doing things was so far out of the norm, that you'd think he had the IQ of a gnat. Then, he'd be able to quote statistics and explain in detail complicated information on something that interested him and you'd wonder how it could be the same brain in that head of his.

Steve was transferred to a new location with his job a few years ago. The training was to last six days and then he was supposed to work a shift by himself. After six weeks, he lacked the skills or confidence to do the job alone. He just couldn't get it. Thankfully, they didn't fire him, but I was really concerned. He doesn't do drugs or drink as his coworkers do, and he faithfully shows up every day so that must account for something.

Sometimes I'm tempted to contact his supervisor and explain to him that Steve has Asperger's, but I don't want to take the chance on him getting fired because of it. They might feel that he is incapable of doing any job. Hopefully, their training has included different personality types and how to motivate them.

Steve seems to respond better to visual instructions than verbal. He downloads manuals for every electronic thing we buy so he can study them on the computer to learn about each product. If I could draw a picture of everything I need him to do around the house, maybe more would get done. Is it laziness or is it AS? It's always hard to tell.

Chapter 10 – Never A Love Song

We were married eight years (I had known him 15 years by then) when I finally discovered the missing piece of the puzzle known as Steve.

It began while talking with a neighbor about his autistic grandson. He shared some of the traits he possessed, which were similar to Steve's. I then called a psychologist friend and asked what she thought. I explained that it seemed like my husband was an autistic adult. She immediately asked if I had checked out Asperger's Syndrome.

I'd never even heard of it before, but quickly did an internet search. What I found was amazing. It described Steve so well! What I knew about him finally had a name. It was a mixed blessing. It was a relief to finally know why Steve was the way he was, but scary because discovery meant I had to face exactly what AS involves.

I don't expect things to ever get better in our marriage, and I am resigned to being lonely for the duration, but at least now I know that Steve cannot help his behavior. He is who he is. He can be sweet, polite and act like an overgrown child most of the time, but he is my husband for better or worse.

No, it is not an ideal situation, and to be honest, if I had known Steve had Asperger's when we'd first met and had known more about it, I would have run as fast as I could in the other direction. I read somewhere that the divorce rate among NT/Aspie marriages is close to 87%, which should tell you something! Marriage to an Aspie is probably one of the toughest things I've ever experienced.

If I was at another place in my life and much younger, I would never put up with the things I do now. I just accept that my emotional and physical needs will never be met as long as I'm Steve's wife.

It does get tiring having to always be the strong one, Mrs. Fix-it, and the one who must maintain some semblance of order in our home.

My Aspie husband is not comfortable being touched and does not reach out to hold or touch me in a loving way. The only time he reaches out to touch me is when he gets a silly grin on his face and gropes me like a pervert for a few seconds as he walks by. That is the extent of our sex life. He's clueless as to what a tender, loving relationship is all about.

As mentioned previously, he prefers to sleep alone. It is tough when married to have to sleep in separate beds, never having any romance, or a spouse put his arms around me to comfort me or just cuddle.

He cannot sense what I'm feeling and needs to be told, which is hard for me to do, because I find it hard to share my own feelings. I was hoping for a husband to be sensitive enough to comprehend my needs. That'll never happen with Steve.

He is a veritable robot who has an obsessive/compulsive habit of kissing me (a quick peck) and saying, "I love you," two or three times before he leaves the house or before he heads to his den, leaving me to be by myself. He has to do it a certain number of times, or else it causes him anxiety like it does the TV character, Monk.

He may love me, but his actions are so mechanical, his seeming affection seems more out of habit than true feelings of love. Maybe he loves me, but it's in a way that leaves me feeling empty.

When a garden isn't carefully tended, the flowers will shrivel and die. Emotionally, that is what has happened to me. Part of me has died, along with any hope for feelings of love or romance. It would take a miracle to resurrect them. I have accepted that my husband is incapable of meeting my needs. He simply cannot empathize with others. Asperger's does not allow him those emotions.

From my experience and from what I've read, most Aspies do not make good spouses and the majority of Aspies never marry. It usually doesn't take a person as long as it did me to find out that an Aspie's personality traits are not suited to that of a marriage partner. They are too focused on themselves and their own needs to ever focus on anyone else. You will find it's all about THEM, rarely, if ever, about you. In my opinion, they make better roommates than husbands or wives.

Throughout all the years we dated, I gradually began to accept Steve as he is, and realized after many disappointments and longings that as long as I was with him there would be no candlelight dinners, no soothing massages or cuddling, no love poems or love notes, no walks in the moonlight, no dancing in the rain, no tender moments just being together or lying in each other's arms, and no flowers and chocolates at random times just because...and there would never be a love song played or sung by the man I call my husband.

I am a caregiver by nature, and being that way, I have a normal tendency to let my own needs take a backseat to the one for whom I'm caring. I go the extra mile in making sure they are happy and treated properly. It is just the way I am and what I do.

And that, my friend, is just a glimpse into what **you** may be doing if you choose to marry someone with Asperger's Syndrome.

Chapter 11 – Hubby's Habits

After it was suggested by a psychologist that my husband might have Asperger's Syndrome, I began making a list of his behavior to confirm the diagnosis.

- Collecting hats/old shoes/coins/clothes/cds/videos/dvds, and things that are out of date
- Hoarding; finds it difficult to get rid of anything whether or not it's old, worn out or nonworking. We have a basement overflowing with things he does not want to throw out.
- When he is driving and we're going together in the same vehicle, he will never even try to clear the clutter from the passenger seat, but leaves his CDs, old receipts, etc. for me to either sit on or remove myself
- Paper fetish (runs through an extremely large amt. of toilet paper and paper towels, napkins, etc. He will not even try to conserve and wastes an enormous amount.
- Before we married, he had started a collection of newspapers that reached almost to the ceiling near the front door. He did the same with soda cans on the kitchen counter.
- Uses hair goop, toothpaste, shampoo, soap, mouthwash in unusually large amts. He buys it in bulk and uses it up fast. He goes through a bar of soap in just a few days, and a huge container of mouthwash in a couple of weeks.
- Is resistant to change. It's difficult for him to try new things as he's quite comfortable with the old ones.
- Does not like to go through a drive-thru restaurant, but must go inside, no matter what the weather.
- If a battery in a clock or smoke detector needs to be changed, he will rarely do it.
- Obsesses about certain things & people: Karen Carpenter and her music, buying/selling houses (spent thousands of dollars on the courses and materials, attended several workshops & has yet to buy or sell even one house); flight simulators, aviation, John Denver, gold panning

- Is more like an adult child needing someone to tell him what to do, yet he refuses to listen unless it's in his normal way of doing things

- He never cries or sheds tears, even when his mother died.

- Often eats with his mouth open and often smacks loudly when he's chewing his food.

- Takes his anger out on inanimate objects (He *has put a hundred little dents in the side of my car by hitting it every time he opens the door of his truck. He also throws things when he's frustrated or angry.*)

- He cannot comprehend that the straightest distance between two points is a straight line. He always chooses the most difficult way of doing things or getting someplace, even with a GPS unit.

- Carries on lengthy conversations with himself daily

- VERY **Rigid**/unchanging behavior (Stressed if his routine changes; Example: *the exact day we were going to buy new fencing for the back yard, he came down with severe back pain; MRI revealed no reason for it. This has happened before*.)

- Chews his fingernails half way down the nail and has his whole life

- Closes doors constantly to shut people out

- Does not value my opinion and has little respect for what I say. If someone else told him the exact same thing, he'd believe it or do what they asked, but not so with me, his wife.

- Goes to the same restaurants, eats the same meals with little variation!

- He cannot ever eat soup without a particular soup spoon. No other spoon will do or else he will get upset and anxious.

- Content to sit in front of the computer for hours watching the same dvd series over & over (Columbo, Emergency, Bionic Woman)

- He will not pet the dog when he walks in the door, but first has to go through one of his many rituals before he will even acknowledge her. Our poor dog is always so excited to see him and can hardly wait for him to pet her, but Steve cannot see that. He cannot depart from his routine of placing the garage door opener, the cell phone, and other items from his pocket in a neat little row on the desk in his office before he turns his attention to our dog.

- Eats his meals alone in his den always with the door closed.
- Little interaction with me, his wife and basically does his own thing
- He's very rough on everything he touches. All damage on my car has

been done by him. He has had to replace brakes on his truck several times, his
heater and a/c unit, arm rest, side mirrors, and many more things inside and
outside the house. He's even poked me accidentally several times in his
awkwardness.

- Lack of organizational skills
- Steve goes about things in a way that uses no common sense and

makes every job much harder than it should be. A ten minute job for anyone else
can be expected to take him a couple of hours or days. A one-day flooring job for
someone else took Steve three months. That was years ago, and he still hasn't put
down the transition pieces to three rooms.

- Procrastination; very little gets done around the house because it's

outside of his normal routine; says "I should do that" or "I meant to do that", but
it's hard for him to even get started on a project

- He has one weekly household chore and still has a problem with it. He

gathers the trash from the wastebaskets and takes it to the curb for pickup. He
only does the basics, never washes the containers, and doesn't check to see if the
wastebaskets are overflowing any other day during the week. Ironically, he'll get
upset if on garbage day the containers have too much in them and will begin to
throw stuff all over the floor even though he'll have to pick it up later.

- He will never, ever balance his checkbook.
- He drinks Diet Coke in excess. He has several cans a day, and also eats

all the wrong things. He has diabetes, but figures since he's taking pills for it, he
can still eat what he wants. He has no self-control when it comes to his diet.

- He refuses to throw away leftovers from his lunch, such as a banana

peel, empty sandwich bags, etc. For years, he has done this. He will leave them
inside his lunch box. He is near trash containers at work where he can easily
pitch them, but has a compulsion to bring it home. He will put the banana peels

neatly folded in an empty sandwich bag, and expects me to throw it away for him when he comes home from work.

- He collects boxes from everything he buys and won't throw them away. I have to make them gradually disappear when he's not around, but there's a never-ending supply, it seems.

- He's sloppy in caring for his car, desk, cameras, and electronic gadgets. He only does what's necessary and what he can get away with. He doesn't help around the house unless I insist.

- If something is spilled or out of place, he will never wipe it up, straighten, or pick it up. As he gets older, I think it's more laziness than AS, but I can never be sure.

- Has a great memory for past events and statistics about people and things that interest him

- It's mainly about "him;" he has little or no empathy for the needs of others, including pets

- Will rarely give a compliment, unless asked directly about whether or not he likes something.

- Though attracted to women who are nice to him, he has little interest in sex.

- Like many autistic adults, he would function best with a caregiver; i.e. to keep his collections and junk from overrunning the house, reminding him to pay bills on time, fix things, etc. He has to be reminded over & over again to do things.

- Is quite comfortable with a messy desk and dresser. Once I clean it, it doesn't take long for him to mess it up again. He will not even try to keep the areas clutter-free.

- When I give him simple instructions or tell him something, two minutes later he will ask a question that had already been answered by what I'd just told him. This is because he is able to focus on one thing at a time. I have to repeat things once or twice in almost every conversation. He just doesn't seem to hear what I'm saying.

- Even with a simple, easy filing system in place, he finds it difficult to put paid bills and paperwork in the proper file. He'd rather throw them on his messy desk.

- When I speak with him, he will often repeat the first words of what I just said.

- He is like an overgrown child. When I try to explain why I'm upset with him, he'll look away and rub his eyes in a circular motion with his fists and elbows up, just like a little boy.

- Though he lacks organizational skills when it comes to projects, he is still able to line up his cell phone, mp3 player, GPS unit, etc. in a neat little row every night when he comes home from work

- He changes his clothes three or more times a day. I am constantly doing laundry, because after work he will not change into his sweats after he showers; instead, he must change into clothing he would wear in public even though no one will see him as he sits in front of the computer. Before bedtime, he changes into sweats. He cannot change this routine, which he's had for years.

A True Confession:

I am ashamed of how I treated my husband for many years before I found out he had AS. I didn't realize he couldn't control his actions as they are a part of his personality. I also didn't realize he took things so literally. I'd often be sarcastic in my replies to him, instead of patient and helpful, when he'd constantly ask what appeared to be stupid questions. I had to learn how to communicate with him in a way he could understand. In fact, I'm still learning.

Marriages are made in heaven.

But, again, so are thunder, lightning, tornados and hail.   --Unknown

Chapter 12 – Not All Bad

I do not wish to give the impression that an NT/AS relationship is unbearable in every respect. Yes, marriage to an Aspie may be tough, but blessings are there, too.

- My Aspie can be trusted to be faithful. He often tells the truth even when it is painful for me to hear it.
- He doesn't take his anger out on me through physical abuse.
- He doesn't smoke or swear, and only drinks on rare social occasions.
- He upholds the laws of the land and is basically an honest man.
- He holds down a steady job due to the grace of God who sees his pure heart.
- He is humble enough to pray with me for our needs, as well as for the needs of others.
- He can be sweet when he offers to pick up dinner so I don't have to cook on weekends.
- When he stops at the gas station for a Coke, he'll sometimes call to ask if I want anything to drink, too.
- Although he puts off doing major jobs around the house, he does mow the lawn and trims the shrubs so the front yard looks nice from the street.
- Although he will never bring me candy or flowers "*just because,*" he will remember certain holidays with a gift and a beautiful card, even if it's mostly out of habit. His mother would constantly nag him about remembering the family's birthdays.
- He'll sometimes offer to check the air pressure in my car tires and will refill the fluids when he checks his.
- When he's out of town, he calls to let me know where he is and how he's doing.
- He was always there with me at the hospital whenever I underwent surgery or other procedures.
- He is not afraid to admit it when he is wrong, and will always say, "I'm

sorry." (*He doesn't usually realize when he's done something to make me really angry, so I have to tell him. When I do, he's remorseful.*)

- He showers, brushes, and flosses his teeth daily.
- If we argue, ten minutes later he's forgotten all about it. He does not seem to ever hold a grudge.
- We rarely have major disagreements--we have what can be called a "comfortable" relationship.

The challenge is to help couples turn "I Do" into "We Can." -- Scott Stanley

Chapter 13 – From My Blog

Food for Thought – Posted on January 5, 2011

My Aspie hubby seems to prefer his food cold. After years of struggling to provide a hot breakfast for him, I made it very clear that it was extremely difficult to cook for him, because he would never come to eat while the food was warm. I'd heat, then reheat, and sometimes have to do it a third time. It wasn't because he didn't know when it would be ready. I'd give him plenty of time, but he still wouldn't appear until 15 minutes to half an hour later. Unless he went through his usual obsessive/compulsive morning rituals, he wouldn't stop to eat. He had to do things in his normal way and couldn't leave anything out. He is an adult and should know how to time things, but he seems incapable of doing so.

Cold eggs and bacon or pancakes and sausage aren't tasty when they're cold, but Steve doesn't seem to care as he never shows up on time to eat them. I've given up trying to plan meals according to his schedule as he's never in a hurry and doesn't care that I'm waiting in the kitchen trying to keep the food warm for him. I really like my crock-pot for that reason. I can put the setting on warm and don't have to worry about Steve showing up. That works for dinner, but I haven't yet figured out how to make it work for breakfast.

A couple of years ago, after telling Steve that I hated cooking breakfast for him for the reasons stated above, he began to eat breakfast at his favorite restaurant. Sometimes we'd go together, but now he just goes by himself on his days off from work. On days he is working, he grabs a cold bowl of cereal and has coffee at work. I'm glad I am no longer a breakfast kitchen slave. There's enough work to do around the house without that added frustration.

I felt Steve was being disrespectful, since I was trying hard to feed him nourishing meals. The least he could do was be there on time to eat them. Then I found out that Steve had Asperger's and that explained his behavior. It also explained why he always has to leave a small amount of food on the plate, too. It is something he's always done and it is part of his routine. He can't stop it now as it's beyond his control.

New Year, Same Old Habits - January 20, 2011

Three weeks into the New Year, but little has changed in Steve's and my relationship.

My car is still not fixed and Steve has not touched it since the first week. It's been over a month. He gets the groceries and I have to instruct him by cell phone on which products to buy. It takes him hours to get the shopping done, because he goes back and forth from one end of the store to the other, even when I try to make it easier for him with an orderly list. He still has so many questions about what he should buy. I thought he might get tired of doing the shopping and fix my car, but he hasn't.

I severely injured my back while shoveling snow a few days before Christmas, and really need to get medical care and an MRI, but have no way of getting there. My symptoms are keeping me in bed much of the day as I cannot stand without wobbling and at times can barely walk. I cannot sleep because I have to get up every two hours to urinate because a disc seems to have collapsed and is pressing on my bladder. Steve just says, "Maybe you should get that checked out." He knows I need a ride, but hasn't offered. His interests and needs always come first.

On garbage day, trash had fallen out of the recycle bins and was laying near the sidewalk. Would Steve pick it up? NO! It is still there and will stay there until I specifically tell him to pick it up. He can be a pig--so unaware, lazy and stubborn if a thing doesn't concern him.

His bathroom is filled with toilet paper rolls that have a remnant of paper left on them. He won't use it down to the end of the roll, but leaves some on. I used to throw them away, but not anymore. If he wants to live that way, I let him.

Steve likes to carry lots of change in his pockets as his dad did when he was growing up. He throws it all over his dresser and no matter how many containers I have nearby, he refuses to put the coins in them. Consequently, change falls all over the place and onto the floor. Early in our marriage, I solved that problem by telling him that any coins that fell on the floor were mine. I have a piggy bank full of the coins I picked up. Now, he only has an occasional lapse, and will at least bend down to pick up those that fall on the floor. He still throws his coins on the dresser, but that is just Steve. He's messy...what can I say?

I've been thinking of getting a new car, since Steve won't work on my old one. Haven't figured out yet how I'll get to the dealer, but will work that out later. I've hesitated to buy a new one before (my car is 16 yrs. old), because all but two dents on my car were put there by Steve. There are about 100 small dents on it where he hit it with his truck door. He also broke a plastic piece that holds the seatbelt. So, 99% of the damage to my car has been done by him.

He has no respect for my things and grinned his Aspie grin when I mentioned it to him. I told him that if I get a new car, I will charge him $100 for every dent he puts in it and won't even give him a key to the car. I don't think that is unreasonable under the circumstances.

Steve does bring in the newspaper in the morning as he heads out the door to work, so that's a good thing. He has other endearing qualities that I know I should dwell on, but right now I'm just back in frustrated mode. When I don't feel well, it'd be nice if I had a husband that would take care of me and recognize what I need. I've learned that T.L.C. is not inherent in an AS male.

The Natives Are Restless – February 13, 2011

I've been concerned that sharing my story has become too negative, and resolve to focus on the more positive aspects of an NT/AS relationship. It's a difficult balance, as I also do not want to paint a picture that makes everything appear so rosy when it definitely is not. It is in no way what you would call a "normal" relationship.

I've heard from both sides and have obviously touched a nerve in many instances. The majority of those who don't have AS have been grateful for me sharing my story and being open to tell it like it is. Those with AS have provided the most negative comments. I know I've been brutally honest, but I'm not going to whitewash the situation. This is my life and experiences, and I chose to tell it from my point of view. NT's need to know what it is they're in for before they charge headlong into a relationship with someone with AS.

One of my biggest regrets is that I don't have all the answers for those who are so frustrated in their NT/AS relationships that they don't know what to do. They long for the time they can escape through divorce, because they can no longer cope with the problems. One dear woman said she literally "hates" her husband and cannot wait to leave him. She stated he is filthy, doesn't work, and won't take care of himself. I feel her pain and sadness.

I don't know what to tell people to make their life better, and it bothers me--a LOT. All I can do is provide sympathy and understanding and a shoulder to cry on. I pray for everyone who writes that they will be given answers as to how to improve their relationship and for them to be happy.

For those who write who have AS, I do not take their comments personally, even though many spew hate at me for sharing the negative traits of my Aspie. On the contrary, they help me understand more about how an Aspie thinks. I'm grateful, for I still have so much to learn.

Valentine's Day is tomorrow. I finally got out of the house for only the second time in two months yesterday. Steve took me to the store where I bought a Valentine card for him. I'll also make him his favorite chocolate cake for dessert. That's about all I can do this year.

My car is still not fixed and Steve hasn't even looked under the hood since week one back in December, but he still says he can't figure out the problem as to why it won't start. I haven't been too concerned as we've had a couple of feet of snow to make me glad to hibernate this winter. With warmer weather coming soon, I really would like to get it fixed so I can get out and about once again.

Thank you to those who have taken time to write and share your experiences, frustrations, and yes, even the hateful comments. We're all on a journey and if we can help each other through it, that is a good thing.

Happy Valentine's Day 2011!

Asperger Wife

Surprise – February 17, 2011

I was absolutely blown away when for Valentine's Day my husband walked in with a large bouquet of mini-carnations in beautiful, pastel colors and then went back out to his vehicle to return with seven big, red, heart-shaped mylar balloons. He also handed me a candy bar and a card.

It is so out of character for him to go all out like that. I know someone must have encouraged him to do it as that is usually what it takes for him to act. I suspect it was a waitress at the restaurant he frequents, or a coworker. In any case, I am really happy with his actions and still surprised. We've been married almost ten years and this was the most he's ever done. He blew off our anniversary last year, so I wasn't expecting much for Valentine's Day. I guess there's always hope that things can get better.

One Step Forward, Two Back – March 2, 2011

The pretty flowers my husband gave me for Valentine's Day have all died and the balloons are deflating. Yes, things are back to normal in our abnormal home.

I'm still without wheels and it's now been almost three months. It's out of Steve's comfort zone to fix my car and since it concerns someone besides himself, he doesn't care.

This past weekend, I'd asked if he could drive me to see our daughter's family as our son's family was visiting there from another state. It's a three to four-hour drive for us from our home.

It is rare that everyone is together at the same time as we all live in different locations in the U.S., hundreds of miles apart.

When I asked Steve to take me, he gave me his typical Aspie stare and said nothing! That meant no way was he going to interrupt his usual Saturday routine. It would have meant a lot to me, but that didn't matter. He hasn't even seen our latest grandbaby and doesn't seem to care.

The older he gets and the longer we're married, things seem to grow worse. We're drifting farther and farther apart. He still stays up late at night, even though he has to get up very early to go to work. He'd rather fall asleep in front of the computer than go to bed. On weekends, he sleeps half the morning away and takes forever to get ready to leave the house. We still go our separate ways. He, to the restaurant, and I escape in housework, books, our pets, and television.

He recently made plans for his own vacation this summer, yet again? He does not include me, so this year I plan to get away by myself. It'd be nice to travel with my husband, but he gives the impression, as always that he'd prefer to be alone.

A few weeks ago, I told him it seems like he's doing less and less all the time to make our marriage work, and he does just enough to squeak by. Early on in our marriage, he used to try so much harder, but now he doesn't care enough to work at it. He takes me for granted and knows I'll still be here when he gets home. He is well aware of the things that bother me, but he won't even attempt to work at them. The Valentine's Day surprises were very nice, but do not make up for daily neglect.

Last weekend, I mentioned that he needed to stop sleeping so late on the weekends and coming home so late in the day. He does little or no upkeep on the house and that needs to change as it's gone on way too long. Many things have needed to be fixed for years. I fix what I can, but there's a lot I'm physically unable to do.

He finally went out and bought a furnace filter and changed it at my urging. It's supposed to be changed every month in winter, and he hadn't done it for five months. He also went out and bought a bathroom ceiling fan that has needed to be replaced for years, but has not even attempted to install it.

Steve's procrastination is maddening. It's been seven years and the floor tile for the bedroom is still not installed and the old carpet has not been taken up. He has had plenty of personal days off to where he could have done the work, but instead sits in front of the computer or heads out the door for most of the day. I know that many husbands procrastinate, but my Aspie does it to the extreme.

As a husband, Steve will not ever comfort me when I'm hurting, protect me in a crisis or look out for my best interests. He postpones making decisions until the last minute, so I have to be the one to take control. I do not believe this is the way God intended marriages to be with the wife having to wear the pants in the family and always be the strong one.

It is so hard to not be negative and to look for the positive things in our marriage. It almost feels like it's crumbling around me and getting worse all the time. If there was a balance, it'd be easier. Right now, things are still lopsided in Steve's favor. He does what he wants, goes where he wants, spends what he wants, and lives more like a bachelor than a married man. I've yet to learn if it's his AS or just his selfishness that controls him.

I'm probably letting him off too easily, because I don't say much about it to him. So, we'll continue to go on this way a while longer until I can't take it anymore and move out, something I ponder quite often these days.

New Discoveries – March 14, 2011

It was a hectic weekend with Steve and his dad trying to install a hot water heater in our basement. Our old one was still under warranty and should have lasted a few more years.. We are now completely without water as the fitting connections are leaking in spite of Steve's best efforts.

He tried hard and worked late into the night on Saturday and Sunday trying to get the pipes hooked up. Sadly, every time he went to try it out, water spurted from almost every connection he had soldered. This happened several times.

He and his dad made several trips to the hardware store with parts that had to be replaced when the first ones didn't work. Again, a supposedly simple project turned into an expensive nightmare.

Tonight they will try again after Steve gets off of his day job. In the meantime, I'm trying to clean the dishes and kitchen counters as well as prepare dinner for tonight with only a bare minimum of water. I'm a Pioneer woman, used to making do with just the bare essentials, so I can rough it for awhile by heating water on the stove and sponge bathing. But…if there is no water to use, that poses a MAJOR problem.

Steve finds this change extremely difficult. It removes him far from his comfort zone and his AS makes it hard for him to adapt to such situations.

When Steve began to complain about all the problems we've been having lately, I tried to explain to him last night that it could be much worse. People in Japan have recently lost loved ones, their homes, jobs, cars, and many are hungry and thirsty due to the devastating tsunami.

We are so very blessed and our trials here are so very small in comparison. I reminded him that we have to keep things in the proper perspective. Life is always filled with problems. If you don't have any, you're probably dead and laying in a graveyard somewhere.

With having no water, I asked Steve to conserve the few bottles of water we had in the fridge as he only needed enough for brushing his teeth. This morning I found that he had used an entire bottle and part of another. All he had to do was rinse his mouth, swish & swallow and spit. That shouldn't have taken but a little. Steve does not know how to conserve. It is not in his vocabulary.

Twice last night, Steve came into the kitchen and asked if there were any paper towels. I said "yes," but he didn't wait to hear my reply as he wiped his wet hands on his pants looking frustrated. I asked him twice why he didn't use the towel in the bathroom, and he wouldn't answer or look at me. The towel was clean and right near the sink, so I have no idea why he wouldn't use it. He HAD to have a paper towel! It seems like the older he gets the more obsessive/compulsive his behavior becomes.

This and That – March 23, 2011

Well, I finally called a plumber to complete the installation of the hot water heater. Poor Steve worked on it for two days under the guidance of his dad. An expensive ($500+) project, but we have hot water, which is a real blessing especially when you've been without it for a few days.

Now the garage door opener is acting up. It's not that old, but the door keeps popping back open when you try to close it. It should still be under warranty, but I doubt if it will be covered, because Steve got upset and try as he did, wasn't able to fix it.

He tried to adjust it, and in frustration, banged on the door, loosening several bolts, some of which fell out. He had to totally disconnect the opener from the door, so it's not working at all. I again hurt my back opening the door manually. It's a BIG, two-car garage door. This is one thing I cannot fix, because I have no way of getting to the store myself to see if the warranty will be honored, or not. Guess it's a good thing my car is still not working. It's going on four months now.

Yes, I'm still without wheels, and it's really getting to me. Warmer weather is here and I hate to be housebound when it's nice outside. I've been working on craft projects and cleaning, but it's nice to get away every now and then, even if it's just to the store.

Something really nice happened to me recently. Last weekend when Steve did the grocery shopping with my guidance via cell phone, he told me he had a surprise for me from the grocery store. This is not normal behavior for Steve.

Well, he came home and unloaded the groceries and I began putting them away. He came in with a second load and asked if I'd found the surprise. He showed me a bag that I hadn't yet opened that contained a package of taffy apples, which are my favorite treat. I can say I was REALLY surprised. Steve just doesn't do things like that.

Steve had such a big grin on his face and said, "I did good, didn't I?" He sure did! It made me happy to know he was happy in giving me a surprise of something I really would like. And those taffy apples were fresh, crunchy and delicious!

Someone must be praying for us, because things like this don't just happen; least not in our NT/AS marriage.

March 29, 2011

I am so proud of Steve even though it took some nagging at first to get the jobs done.

He fixed the garage door last weekend so it's working well.

He got the groceries with minimal help.

And another job that he would normally postpone for ages was completed quickly.

It really makes things easier when I don't have to do everything around the house. That is a constant source of contention around here. It was good that I was unable to complete the jobs myself for it gave Steve a sense of accomplishment in finishing them and doing them well.

And…I'm happy that my car is at the repair shop and should be ready to go today. I was able to miraculously start it and get it there myself. It was the starter that caused the problem.

Here We Go Again – March 31, 2011

After a series of highs, we're back to the lows.

With my car running once again, I decided to switch parking spaces in the garage with Steve's vehicle. It makes more sense, since my car would be easier to walk around and you could reach the door easier, otherwise, the side door cannot be opened. Steve has to then squeeze in a small space to get in and out of his truck, which makes it easier for him to bang up my car, which he's been doing almost daily for years.

I took the time and effort to move bicycles, a gas grill, and several other things to the opposite side and parked my car in the space where Steve usually put his. I thought he would understand the change and why it was necessary. Well, I thought wrong. You can't mess with a man with Asperger's and his comfortable, unchanging routine.

Steve came home from work and struggled to get his truck in the garage, though it should have been quite easy since I had cleared the space for him. He wasn't coming in the house for a long time, and backed in and out several times. When I came out to ask what was wrong, he began pouting and said he was just going to park outside from now on.

I was so frustrated and told him he was acting like a baby just because he didn't have his familiar spot. He didn't care that the way I switched things made it more convenient. He just couldn't tolerate the change. That meant more to him than anything else.

Last night...same thing happened. This time, he stayed outside twice as long and was pouting and talking to himself yet again. I again went out to talk with him and since he couldn't handle the change and wouldn't even consider the reasoning behind it, I told him I'll let him have his way, yet again, and would move everything back so he could park in his spot that blocks the door & bangs my car.

So, today I will be switching things back before Steve gets home from work. I don't know why I even bother to make things better for us.

To make matters worse, I walked in to Steve's office this morning when he was on the computer, and there was good old, but long dead, Karen Carpenter on the screen. He is still obsessed with her and just won't let it go. Now how do you think that makes an Asperger Wife feel?

Once again I have to bite the bullet and let Steve have his way, but sometimes I wonder if it's really worth it. There are good things about our marriage, but the bad often get in the way of calling it a truly happy one.

What are your frustrations with your mate? How do you resolve them? Or do you just suffer in silence and let them have their way?

Spring Has Sprung – April 16, 2011

This past week my husband's truck needed to be repaired and he asked me to give him a ride to and from work. I'd been rationing my gas since it is very expensive these days, but told him I'd do it. After thinking about it, I couldn't resist mentioning to him that when my car was not working and I needed his help, he did not provide it. That left me without a car for almost four months. He immediately blurted out in a pouting manner, as is his custom, "Well, okay then. I'll just walk to work."

I'm trying to help him realize that as a married couple, we're supposed to help each other whenever there is a need. Unfortunately, in our relationship, it's a bit one-sided as he's quite self-absorbed. If he doesn't get his way, he'll blurt out something totally to the extreme. When he does, I get upset and tell him to stop acting like a baby.

As mentioned more than a few times in this site, his behavior and conversation seems motivated by anxiety and stress in his life. He keeps things inside and since he rarely shares his fears and problems with me, the only way I know when he's on overload is to listen outside the door when he's having one of his daily conversations with himself.

Steve did get his truck fixed the next day, and just took a flex day from work to get it done. I gave him a ride to places he wanted to go while it was being repaired.

* * * * *

I've been busy tackling spring cleaning at our house this past week and am really making headway. I know it's a struggle for Steve to part with anything, but I did ask him if I can get rid of some things and explained that it would make life easier for both of us. He didn't give me a definite answer, but at least he will have time to adjust before the charity truck picks up our donations in a couple of weeks.

Once he sees the benefit of more space in the house and basement, he seems happy and doesn't even miss items that are gone. It's thinking about parting with them that makes him anxious. I just have to make sure if I get rid of anything, it's done in small steps and ALWAYS when he's not home. That way, he is better able to deal with it.

I'm REALLY enjoying have more space to do my crafts and not have to work around a cluttered house and basement. It gives me a sense of well-being and I know Steve is happy, too, even if he doesn't show it.

April is National Autism Awareness Month – April 26, 2011

The United States recognizes April as a special opportunity for everyone to educate the public about autism and issues within the autism community.

Know the Signs: Early Identification Can Change Lives

Autism is treatable. Children do not "outgrow" autism, but studies show that early diagnosis and intervention lead to significantly improved outcomes.

Here are some signs to look for in children:

- *Lack of or delay in spoken language*
- *Repetitive use of language and/or motor mannerisms (e.g., hand-flapping, twirling objects)*
- *Little or no eye contact*
- *Lack of interest in peer relationships*
- *Lack of spontaneous or make-believe play*
- *Persistent fixation on parts of objects*

Frustrating & Fascinating AS – May 6, 2011

I bought a sign for Steve's office a year or two ago that I myself feel like using today. It is a picture of a bulls-eye and across the bull's-eye in large letters are the words **"BANG HEAD HERE."**

The other day Steve mentioned that he wants to put a workbench in the garage and that he'd like to now switch parking places in the garage as I had suggested to him before. (**Bang head here.**) *When we do, Steve will have to* be the one to move everything around as I stubbornly refuse to do it again.

I began thinking that Steve always seems to initially disagree with my suggestions and won't budge to do them, even though they are made with common sense reasoning. Then, out of the blue, days, weeks or even months later, he will often change his mind and decide to do the very thing I asked in the first place. It's as if it suddenly seemed to make sense to him. When he does come to that point, however, he has an entirely different reason for actually doing the thing, thereby making it "his" idea. Maybe that allows him to be comfortable with the decision to change something in his normally rigid routine.

The more I learn about Asperger's, the more fascinated I am with it. It is such a complex thing and each person who has it is so unique. One thing I know for a fact is that God did not make a mistake when he created individuals with AS. They have a special place in His heart, and it is up to us to make room for them in our hearts, as well.

Peace to all.

I Dreamed a Dream - May 7, 2011

I want to share with you a dream I had on February 26, 2009. The dream was so vivid that I remembered it clearly once I woke up from sleep.

My husband, Steve, and I and our little dog were in an automobile. Steve was driving and the dog and I were in the backseat with me sitting directly behind Steve.

Steve decided to take a treacherous route onto a mountain ledge that was very unstable and rocky. To the left was a high rock wall and on the right was a rock wall that went straight down for miles. The ledge was barely wide enough for a car and was extremely dangerous. Understandably, I was quite fearful and asked Steve why he took that route and said we shouldn't have gone that way.

As we inched forward, the ledge behind us crumbled and we couldn't go back. The ledge ahead was also crumbling and the car began to tilt. I tried to grab the door handle to my left so I could hold on and stay in the car, but didn't. I couldn't find anything else to grab, either, so I just let go and fell out. As I did, Steve said, "Oh!" turned towards me, and just watched me fall. He did nothing to help me.

Before I fell, we couldn't turn around in the car and couldn't back up. We had gotten to a point where we couldn't move forward, either. We were slowly inching along trying to make it to smooth road that we hoped would be ahead, but were stuck on the rocky ledge until I fell out. Then I woke up.

You can draw your own conclusions from this dream, but I know it clearly defines our NT/AS relationship.

I always take a backseat to Steve's wants and wishes. He does the driving in our relationship as indicated by my not sitting next to him in the front seat, which would put us on an equal level.

When Steve does things he makes them so much more difficult than they have to be, signified by the rocky road he chose to take in the dream.

With the road crumbling, I feel it meant our marriage was in trouble, but we couldn't back up and start over, so we had to go on in spite of the difficulties that lay ahead.   We were stuck in the middle of a bad situation.

With the road ahead crumbling, as well, it caused the car to tilt as we attempted to move, so it didn't look promising that we'd make it to our final destination safely. That was evidenced when I fell out of the vehicle and Steve did nothing to stop me. I was on my own in the dream, as in our life.

It's quite sad when you think about it.

It Took a Bribe - May 12, 2011

Ahhh, it's another spring day. The leaves are on the trees, flowers and veggies have been planted, and stormy weather has hit the Midwest. Inside our home, it's the same old situation with the same old problems, more or less.

Steve has his vacation all planned for late in July, and when he told me about it, I said I wouldn't mind his going as long as he took a day off work before then to finish painting the bedroom, pulling up the old carpet, and putting down new floor tile.

I've had the tile since 2004, so I think it's long overdue. If I could do the work myself, I would, but I can't, so it was up to Steve. It was giving him almost three months notice to get 'er done, which is more than enough time for him to adjust to the idea.

When he asked if he could take my Netbook with him on his trip, I said sure. Then I made him a deal he couldn't refuse. I told him I'd give it to him to keep if he finished the bedroom project before he left on his vacation. He accepted the bribe, which I figured he would. The Netbook is like new and has nice accessories that Steve, himself, gave me for Christmas, so he really likes them.

It took him a couple of weeks, but he then asked for an entire week off from work, since he has several weeks vacation time coming. He is hoping to work on the bedroom then. For anyone else, the project could be finished in a day or two as the bedroom is small. For Steve, that never happens. I'm praying he'll get it done in the week he's off. He's so pokey that by the time he starts on a project, the day's half over.

When it's not a work day, Steve will stay up very late and sleep till 10 or later, and then he goes to a restaurant to eat breakfast and hang out, as usual. By the time he gets home to do anything, it's already mid-afternoon. That only leaves a few hours to work on a project.

Maybe I should take a vacation while he's working on the bedroom. From past experience, I know I will get so frustrated when I see Steve hauling all the furniture out of the room, when all he has to do is push it to one side while he's working. He always makes things harder for himself than he has to. When will I ever learn to just not even watch him at all, but praise him when and if the job gets done?

Angry and Sad – May 27, 2011

There must be a full moon this week. The other morning I awoke at 4:00 a.m. to hear a neighbor yelling at her husband before she left the house for work with the slam of a door. Later the same day, the neighbor on the other side of us was teaching his autistic grandson to mow the lawn. Yelling and profanity could be heard.

The man was cursing the boy, who is around 12 years of age, at the top of his lungs, stating that the rows weren't straight. Forget about his grandson's feelings or self-esteem, the grass was more important!!! I felt very bad for the child.

I'm still feeling sad for the boy who was adopted by our neighbor as a baby as his mother (our neighbor's daughter) had mental problems. So our neighbor is both grandfather and father to the boy who attends special classes for autistic students. His father once told me that he'll never be able to live alone and care for himself because of his autism.

The boy wasn't physically beaten, so I couldn't call child protective services, but I'm sure this incident has bruised his psyche. His grandfather is 70 yrs. old, and his wife is in her sixties. I know he is stressed about their possibly not being around to care for the boy and wants to teach him how to do things, but the boy will have an even more difficult time learning if he continues to be so impatient with him.

Observing that incident did make an impact on me as I find myself being more patient with my husband. It seems to be having a positive effect and we're getting along better. That may change, however, as he's off next week and will begin working on the bedroom. Pray for us! 😊

Bedroom Project – Day 2 – May 29, 2011

Yesterday, Steve began working on the long-awaited bedroom project. I'm so happy he chose to start it on the first day of his vacation, rather than waiting until the last I guess Steve really wants that Netbook, which I am giving him to keep if he completes the job before he goes on his vacation in late July.

As expected, Steve wanted to clear the entire room before he began tearing up the old rug. He removed the door from the bedroom, which he did not need to do, and then proceeded to haul furniture from the room into our living room. He said it would only be for a couple of days. I hope so.

We had only minor confrontations during the day, which shows we're both making progress. Through the years, I've come to know what to expect whenever Steve does any kind of project, so I was much calmer this time. I refrained from getting upset when he again made more work for himself. As long as the job gets done, I'll be happy.

I tried to help as much as I could, but basically Steve did the majority of the work himself.

He got off track a bit when he felt it was more important to work on the ceiling fan than to begin painting, but again, I had to back off to avoid a futile argument.

As I type this, Steve is eating breakfast at his favorite restaurant, even though I'd had coffee and food ready for him this morning at home. He refused it as he couldn't interrupt his normal routine of going out to eat.

He did rise early, only because he set his bed in the middle of the family room and our pets and I are early risers. I had to walk past him to let the animals outside. Our dog, seeing him there, couldn't help but jump on the bed and try to kiss his face. Once awake, he decided to get up a few hours earlier than usual. Hopefully, he should be back home and working on the project much earlier than an afternoon start.

So far, all pictures, etc. have been removed from the walls, the rug is up and the floor is cleared. The ceiling fan work is still unfinished, but I was impressed that as much got done as it did. Steve bundled up the old rug, took it outside, where it's ready for trash pickup in a few days.

All in all, I think the project is going well. I only hope it will be finished tomorrow. That would allow Steve the rest of the week to enjoy relaxing. He'd have six days to lay around and do nothing. I think he'd like that. 😊

BEDROOM PROJECT – DAY 5 – June 1, 2011

Steve did a beautiful job on painting the bedroom and we're both happy with the colors selected for the walls. He's definitely taking his time and doesn't seem in a big hurry to complete the project. That is his normal way of doing things, so I'm not surprised. He is a perfectionist in many ways when it comes to doing any kind of work around the house, but it's frustrating to see him work while getting to the finish line.

Today, for example, he was measuring the room for a long time, which did absolutely nothing to help things. It was unnecessary, but he felt he should do it because that's what he's done in the past. The other day, I found him sitting on the floor talking to himself just thinking about what should be done. He wasted half a day just doing that. I had bought the tile in 2004, and knew I had bought enough to cover the entire floor with extras in case of mistakes. All the measuring was done in 2004, and the room hasn't changed in size, of course. Steve still felt the need to waste a couple of hours trying to figure out if there was enough tile. Of course there was, but he had to be sure. 😊

Every other room in the house is filled with furniture and things from the bedroom. I can hardly wait until the bedroom is finished and things are put back in order. It may be another couple of days, however.

Today, Steve's putting plywood down on the floor. He only began working on it in the afternoon, so I doubt if he'll get to lay the tile today or not. If he'd started early, he could have easily finished up today.

We have been getting along pretty well, all things considered. I am chilling out more and nagging less. Griping to him doesn't help as Steve moves at his own pace and he will get the job done in his time and it will be done well.

TRYING TO0 BETTER UNDERSTAND MY ASPIE – June 8, 2011

The bedroom project is pretty much completed with the exception of a few small things left to do, such as pulling up the old rug in the closet and laying tile there, as well as hanging curtain rods. Those things shouldn't take but about an hour to do, total. In Aspie time, it'd probably be half a day, or more.

This project gave me a better understanding of my Aspie and why he's so meticulous when it comes to doing any kind of project. A rare thing, but he opened up and shared with me that the people he worked for years ago would really get upset if a job wasn't done precisely the way they wanted it to be completed.

Steve was always afraid to make a mistake because if he did, they'd yell at him and threaten to take money from his paycheck. Therefore he took painstaking measures to make sure that didn't happen. That also explains why Steve is never in a big hurry to start a project or finish it. So, it's not just Asperger's that causes his procrastination, but his life experiences.

On another matter, I have questions for Aspies out there who may be reading this. Are you able to feel jealousy? Do you know what it is? Are there any emotions that you cannot feel or comprehend?

It seems my Aspie doesn't ever get jealous, and doesn't even know what it involves. He can understand the concept of right and wrong when it comes to adultery, but doesn't realize that I can still get feelings of jealousy when he is overly friendly towards other women. I feel there are boundaries that shouldn't be crossed if you're married, and he's walking a fine line.

I'm bringing this up, because the husband of one of his women friends passed away suddenly. The wake was last night. Steve went, I felt, because other women friends would be there, too. He took twice as long to get ready as he normally does, which is a long time. It was almost as if he was preparing for a date he was so dressed up. Although I didn't say anything to him about it, I was upset.

It was a good thing he was paying his respects, but I do wonder why he went to so much trouble to look his absolute best. Things like that do cause me to get jealous, especially since he doesn't put forth much effort to make our own relationship work.

TEMPER TANTRUM – June 19, 2011

It happened again yesterday. Steve was overwhelmed because of a stressful situation and began to throw things around his office in frustration. I reacted as well by calling him a baby. It seems that's the first word out of my mouth whenever he does. I know...not a nice thing to do. I just expected that by his age, which is nearing the half century mark, he'd have learned to better control his anger.

Steve was upset because of what happened the day before as he pulled out of our driveway on his way to work. He backed into the neighbor's car that was parked (illegally) across from our driveway. He put a huge dent in the door. Thankfully, the neighbors said the car was old and had already been damaged anyway so they weren't angry about it. Instead, they said they would try and have a friend pull the dent out, and if that didn't work, they may have to get a new door. They were trying to make sure that Steve wouldn't have to pay more than necessary, which was really nice of them.

I did not berate Steve for backing into the car, but mentioned that because he is getting so little sleep during the work week, he is not as alert as he should be. I get frustrated knowing that Steve still stays up late and expects to get by on four or five hours sleep a night. He will not listen to me and continues to act foolishly.

This latest incident was not the first. You see, he has had a couple of other insurance claims and a few moving violations. He is not driving as much as before because his job no longer requires it, but he still needs to be alert at work and when he is on the road getting to and from there.

Any suggestions as to how to make Steve realize he needs to take better care of himself and get to bed at a decent hour? He just stares at me whenever I try to mention it to him, and continues to do what he wants, as always.

Depression – June 26, 2011

After living so long with an Aspie, I think I'm the one with mental problems and a martyr complex for I continue to subject myself to emotional and physical neglect. I often wonder why I bother to stay.

Steve just keeps moving farther and farther away from me. For my sanity, I realize I have got to get out of the house, maybe take a vacation, and maybe live separate lives in separate places. I'm tired, depressed and though I love Steve, it's just too much.

I have no outlet for my frustrations and it affects my physical and emotional well-being. And...the MOST frustrating thing about it is that Steve DOESN'T or ISN'T able to even care. He is oblivious to anyone beside himself. He is in his own little world, and only ventures my way when it comes for me doing something for him, such as cutting his hair, cooking his meals, fixing his lunch, etc.

Sighhh...no wonder I'm depressed.

No Protector - July 4, 2011

A couple of years ago I had a sad revelation about my Asperger husband. He would never be the strong one in our relationship, and he would never be the one to protect me in a crisis.

We've been married ten years now and it's been a rather rocky road as new discoveries about his Aspie behaviors were (are) gradually being revealed over time. Each negative thing I learn makes me sad, because it just confirms the reality that my marriage will never be what you would consider "normal."

I often regret that my husband will never put his arms around me to comfort me if I'm hurting, because he cannot comprehend my feelings. He operates in a different way and though he may care, he is unable to show it through displays of affection.

I've stated before that my husband is more like a robot with his obsessive behavior patterns and I guess I have become one, too. I go through the motions of being a happy, contented wife when in actuality, my feelings have been pushed aside so long that I feel numb.

Acceptance is key in staying married and doing it without feeling like a martyr or making my husband feel less than a man. I try to focus on his good traits, such as his being polite, his good work ethic, his honesty, and the other positive reasons I married him in the first place. If you look for the negative, it is always there to be found, so it's best not to dwell on it.

If you are involved with an Aspie, how do you cope and what makes you stay (or feel like leaving) the relationship? If you have left, are you happier for having done so or do you regret not sticking around longer trying to make it work?

Frustrated to No End - July 5, 2011

Linda, I want to welcome you to the Asperger Wife site.

Thank you so very much for taking time to share your story. It saddens me to know there are so many more of us out there who haven't yet connected the dots and don't even realize that their mate suffers from the dreadful Asperger's. They know something's not right, but can't put their finger on exactly what it is. Some may never know and suffer in silence.

I can relate to your experiences of being married to an Aspie so very much. When you wrote "*The emotional and mental torture is enough to send me to an asylum! My hope is to get to a place, with God's help, that I don't act like a victim, use negative coping, and have a quarterly meltdown. Maybe I can act like his other wife - indifferent, no emotion, no intimacy - and accept* his work around the house and his paycheck. And I can find fulfillment elsewhere..." it showed me that you've come to that point through a process of neglect and hurt. Your needs are not being met and these are coping mechanisms you use to help you survive.

I've done the same. Little by little my self-esteem was being chipped away by my Aspie's lack of intimacy and inability to function like a normal husband. I eventually became indifferent because after trying every way I knew to change things for the better, I realized my Aspie marriage will not ever improve and there will never be the romance in my life that would make me a happy wife. My Aspie seems content without it, because I don't think he comprehends what romance is. He seems to lack such feelings and can't (or won't) pick up on mine, either.

When you wrote one of the reasons you stay is financial, I can also relate to that. Also, since I'd been married twice before, I don't want to be considered a "three-time loser." I've finally made a decision that I have to do something. I cannot go on like this and keep my sanity. Instead of getting a divorce, however, I am looking into escaping through buying a small house in a quiet town near my daughter's family and using it as an investment, as well as a getaway home for vacations.

I do wonder if I will get so used to life alone and knowing I can make it by myself that I won't want to come back. It's a dangerous place to be, but my Aspie seems to prefer being alone anyway. We sleep apart, and he goes his own way. I mostly see him when he emerges from his man cave to come out to get the meals I've prepared for him.

I also realize that he has little concern for things that concern me, and he's backing away so far that there's really little reason to stay other than the fact he pays the utility bills and the mortgage. I continue to pay for my own needs, such as car expenses, clothes, house extras, part of our groceries.

He used to pay for my cell phone, but now I'm paying for that, because when we changed carriers, he asked if I still wanted one. He is not that stupid and has to know that it's a necessity if I ever have a car problem when away from home. I realize that he just didn't want to pay for it, so I told him "no" and went out and bought a trac phone for emergencies.

Things he used to do when pretending to be a good husband early in our marriage, he no longer does. He used to bring me breakfast from McDonald's on weekends, and we got into a pattern that we'd eat fast food so I wouldn't have to cook on Sat. & Sun. I cook five days a week, prepare his lunches, too, and rest on weekends.

He gradually stopped getting breakfast for me, but began to head out alone to his favorite restaurant on the weekends. Then he would sleep so late that by the time he got done at the restaurant, it was late in the afternoon, so he stopped bringing home lunch for me as well. So, we're down to two dinner meals on Sat. & Sun. that he will bring home. I feel it's just because he's trying to see how much he can "not do" and still stay married.

He dents my car, destroys several other things of mine by carelessness, and he does little around the house but heads out to stores to look around on weekend afternoons. He still will not take out the overflowing garbage or empty the dehumidifier in the basement. Those are the only two things I ask him to do on a regular basis. I've begun doing those tasks myself because I don't like tripping over garbage when I'm trying to keep a clean kitchen and things stored in the basement need to be protected from humidity, so I have to keep the dehumidifier empty.

My bad back is aggravated when I lift anything heavy like the container filled with water from the dehumidifier, but he doesn't care. I don't know if he's just lazy or if it's his Asperger's that make him not want to do it. He just doesn't do anything to try and improve our marriage.

He refuses to cut the grass in the back yard very often even though he knows I like to sit out there and it's too "buggy" when the grass is high. He also won't cut the grass because he doesn't like to mow around the small trees I planted there.

He used our joint account to purchase an expensive gas trimmer, but won't use it in the backyard. He takes care of the front yard well, because people see it and might otherwise complain. We have a tall fence that blocks out the view of the backyard, so he doesn't care. We have mulberry trees that need branches cut back to keep mulberries from staining our patio and new back deck. With a torn rotator cuff, I've had to try and cut back the branches--a job that Steve should be doing.

We had two vacations together (both planned by him) early in our marriage, but now he goes alone. He asked if I'd come with him, but he knows I have to stay behind to care for our pets. They aren't allowed where he chooses to go. When we vacationed together, I took the one pet we had at the time with us as we were mainly going camping and it worked out well.

Well, I could go on, but it won't do much good other than to release pressure from the build up of pent-up feelings of resentment, anger, and hurt that come from living with an Aspie husband.

Thanks again for sharing, and I hope others will join in and express their thoughts and let us know what they're experiencing in their Aspie relationships.

71

July 18, 2011 – Monday

I must apologize that I have not been keeping up with this website as I should. Occasionally, I must focus on other things besides Asperger's. I've also been very busy lately.

The house hunt is going full speed ahead. At this point, my husband is not sure if I'm leaving him or if I'll return. He hasn't said much about my buying a house, but seems to be okay with it. I try to include him in the details and ask his opinion. He hasn't said much and I have to pry to get him to open up and say what's really on his mind.

I've also been busy writing a book and it should be ready for publication within the next month. A while back someone suggested I write one, and I took their advice. Thank you whoever you are. 😊

Alone, I read your latest reply and I try to understand how you are feeling, but it appears you just don't want to change for it's too much work. I know it's difficult, but would you try if you knew your mate would be leaving you?

My Aspie begged me to give him a second and a third chance, swearing he'd try harder to work at our marriage. He tried for awhile, but then settled into his usual pattern of behavior, and that's where we are now. That is why I am more focused on my own needs instead of his at this time. I've given up expecting things to be different. It's either stay and put up with him as he is, warts and all, or move out and not have to deal with it day in and day out.

I plan on staying away for weeks at a time once I find the right house. It will take me that long to unwind and recharge. He's welcome to come and join me, but I seriously doubt he will. He seems to prefer being alone. Well, I do, too, considering the alternative.

July 26, 2011

It's a peaceful morning on our home. My Aspie husband is out of town this week enjoying a vacation alone. He calls daily to let me know how he's doing and is having a nice time. He's happiest doing his own thing.

I, too, have begun to relish my own independence and am doing what I can to create my own happiness. In spite of physical limitations, I am reaching beyond my four walls to finally do things that I've wanted to do for a long time. If I'm miserable, I'm mainly the one to blame. If I want to be happy, I need to take steps myself to achieve that goal as I cannot depend on my Aspie to do it.

Today I am making an official offer on a house and hopefully it will be accepted. It causes anxiety when I begin thinking of going off on my own when there's so much to do on a daily basis at our main home. It will be twice as much work, but hopefully I can return feeling refreshed and ready to take on the challenge of housework and caring for my husband again. I'm hoping he will be more appreciative of all that I do for him, but I don't count on it. Absence is supposed to make the heart grow fonder, but I'm not sure if that works for Aspies or not. We'll see.

To those of you who are in a relationship with an Aspie...*what are you doing to take care of yourself?* It is unhealthy to be under constant stress with no form of release. You may find peace if you can find a way to do things that make you happy and change your focus from constantly trying to please your Aspie while neglecting your own health & happiness. There should be a healthy balance.

One more thing...I want to welcome the new members of this site. I'm glad you are here!

July 31, 2011

I'd like to thank everyone who regularly view this blog and website and who contribute by posting their thoughts and feelings. It will help us all to better understand one another.

This week has flown by so quickly. My Aspie husband will be returning home tomorrow from his vacation trip. He has called me once or twice a day to update me on things he's seen and places he's been. Ironically, it's about the only time we really have good conversation. It's most likely because he's sharing about what interests "him."

I've been quite at peace since Steve's been gone and functioned quite well without him. Of course, his being with me is almost like not having him there anyway since he's usually in his office in front of the computer with the door shut.

The sellers accepted my offer and the closing on my own little house will be sometime in the next two weeks. I'm still a bit anxious when it comes to the idea of caring for two houses, but I have done it before so I can do it again. I admit I also am a bit anxious as to how Steve will react when I'm gone for weeks at a time. Since he seems to prefer being alone to doing things with me, he shouldn't mind it...really.

I had wanted Steve to come to the closing with me so he could see the house, but he has been less than enthusiastic about it. It would also be a help to use his truck to move things instead of cramming them in to my compact car. I'm not counting on his helping with that, either, due to his past behavior. I may have to rent a truck and drive it myself, which I've also done before.

I thought I could count on my Aspie for many things when we were dating and first married, but now he's so set in his ways that he pretty much only does what he wants and what will mainly benefit him. We don't have a marriage, but are house mates whose lives occasionally collide.

Saturday, August 6, 2011

Another day in Aspie town... It's a gloomy morning and not a pleasant start to what I'd hoped would be a nice weekend. Steve is working half a day today and has already left for his favorite restaurant hangout to eat breakfast before he heads to the job site.

There are several important matters that have to be handled and Steve is dragging his feet yet again on taking care of them. These are things I can't do myself; otherwise they would have been done long ago. I've stressed to him the importance of handling them immediately, but he just ignores me.

I know he's been busy, but he could have allowed one day of his vacation to take care of pressing matters. He is such a procrastinator. It bothers me when he has to pay late charges on overdue bills when he has the money in his account to cover them. He just doesn't take time to pay them. Our new gutters are filled with debris that has been left after several storms hit this summer, and yet he won't take time to clean them. Instead, our deck is littered with the gunk overflow. For that reason, a mess is tracked on to the floor whenever we or our pets come in the door, so it's a constant struggle to keep things neat.

Maybe I'm just depressed due to the weather and the fact that there will be a delay in the closing on my house due to a personal problem of the realtor's. I'd hoped to move in by mid-August, but now it may not be until September or later.

Steve's lack of enthusiasm about helping me with the move or anything for that matter just makes me glad I will soon have a place to get away from him and his "I don't care about you or what you do" attitude. If I don't even have a chair to sit on in my new house, at least I'll have peace.

Since Steve refuses to help me with transporting things to the new house, in my mind I have decided to stay away a day longer than originally planned for every day he aggravates me. I know...I can be gone for a very long time. :-)

It'll be nice not having to carefully study every word that I say so that my Aspie will understand the point I'm trying to make. Also, I won't have to repeat myself over and over and/or nag Steve to do a myriad of other things that he's neglected to handle for many years.

Basically, Steve does what he wants. Period. His only focus is on himself and his needs. My opinion doesn't count, and my reasoning doesn't make sense to him. Occasionally, he offers to do something small for me, but the majority of the time, he does not want my life to interfere with what he has planned for his. Sighhhh. What a waste of what could have been a good marriage.

August 12, 2011

NT's, this question is for you. Is your Aspie an angry person? My Aspie gets upset often, but more often than not, it is with himself and inanimate objects. He rarely aims his anger towards me, but expresses his irritation with me through his body language. He mostly shuts down and continues to talk to himself in another room. He doesn't rage, calculate, or order me around. Does yours?

The reason I'm asking is that this poem below seems to describe this woman's husband as someone who is mean and angry. I don't think all Aspies are mean, spiteful and angry. My Aspie is quite docile really, compared to the person described below. He is not intentionally hateful, but his behavior is just downright aggravating and unintentionally hurtful quite often.

The poem below was written by an anonymous author, but I wish I could have discovered her name to give her credit for it. I'm sure it was written in one of the many lonely moments of her life as an Asperger wife. She describes the average NT/AS marriage so very well.

My Asperger Marriage.

From the beginning awareness that something is wrong
A relationship that's fundamentally flawed and limited
Intimacy eludes every effort
Subconscious grief
Cold reality slowly settles in my heart
A loneliness that shouldn't be
A relationship that consumes every facet of my being
Yet abandons my basic human need to belong
Controlled, yet abandoned

Dominated, yet neglected

Needed, yet no-one

Promised, yet nothing

Diagnosis acknowledges what I already know

It is everything I thought, yet more

Blackness engulfs my soul like a shadow with form

Crushing out every whisper of hope

Or anticipation of something better

At first a relief

A book of answers for decades of questions

Reassurance of my own sound state of mind

Acknowledgement of all the hard work and pain

Just keeping it all on track

No healing, no solution, no remedy

A new way to live

A new way to love

New rules for ordinary things

Strategies for daily functioning

Mechanical methods

Altered responses

For better or for worse, in sickness and in health

All of these, all at once

A different state of being

A different definition of marriage

Bound, but alone

Alongside, but solitary

The sense of loss is engulfing

Loss of hope

Loss of dreams

Grief for what will never be

No union of two free minds and souls

Bound in love, care and respect

It's not like that and never will be

One free mind

One with sharp corners

One soul that lives and breathes with love and spontaneity

One that calculates and orders, hides, fears and rages

No effort on my part can change his state of mind

My love doesn't warm him

My care doesn't reach him

My personality doesn't win him

My feelings and opinions don't sway him

A different life

- Anonymous

TGIF – August 19, 2011

I'm posting just a quick note early on a Friday morning. I'm in a rush today as the closing day on my house is finally here, but wanted to stop and welcome the new members to the site. I'm so glad you are here!

My hubby did a surprisingly sweet, unexpected thing the other day and it made me quite happy. Then, Asperger's shortly thereafter reared its ugly head and the usual problems appeared along with it. That's the way it goes--ups and downs. I guess life is that way even without AS in it, but somehow it seems harder when it is in the picture.

I wish you all a very happy day and a super weekend. Take some time for yourself and do something for YOU for a change.

Peace...

August 25, 2011

Good morning, everyone.

The sun is shining and it feels more like September than late August with temps dropping down into comfortable 60's and 70's in my neck of the woods.

My head is spinning over how I'm going to balance living in two places, decorate a home and how I'm going to do it without a truck, pay for taxes, etc. and how my Aspie husband is going to react when I tell him I may be away for weeks, possibly months at a time. With Steve's resistance to any changes in his normal routine, the price of food, gas and utilities so high and it all being my responsibility, it's not going to be easy, but the end result should be worth it. I will have a place where I can go to unwind and forget for a time about living with a man who is in his own little world.

After several weeks of hearing me talk about it, Steve began to finally express some interest in the new house, but only after I kept pressing the issue about how I'd really like for him to see it. He says he wants to see it, and talks about maybe in a couple of weeks doing that, but he's shown more enthusiasm for the strawberry pie I made for dessert than for actually wanting to make the trip there.

I'm not going to say another thing about it to him. His resistance is typical Steve behavior. Steve mainly cares about Steve and what will benefit him. He can't see how the house will fit into his plans.

This morning I went out to get the paper and came outside as Steve was preparing to leave for work. He was very upset about something, but Lord knows what it could be. With Steve, it's hard to tell. He used profanity and I told him that I hope he wasn't using the word I thought I'd heard him say. He said, "Oh, well..."

Profanity is not commonly used in our home. I guess he hears it so often at work that it is rubbing off on him. I don't want to hear it, however, and he knows that.

Sometimes I feel like screaming. It is depressing that, although I'm the supposedly normal one, my life will never really be normal. I will never have a real, romantic, passionate love affair with my husband, never experience rainbows and brilliant colors of a marriage with real love and give and take, and never have more than a "blah" existence as long as I'm married to Steve. I guess that should be enough, but since so many things are lacking, I can't help but feel regret.

So, again, I strive to make my own happiness, since no one, especially Steve, is going to do it for me.

September 2, 2011

Well, my living room is filled with things I'm taking to the new house and I'm preparing to leave sometime next week. Our anniversary will be celebrated apart, but I don't care. It's just another day. My gift to Steve will be my leaving, since he seems to prefer being alone. This way he can have the house to himself and won't have me there to bother him and press him for an occasional conversation.

Steve has been working overtime, but said when I'm gone he will come home earlier. Go figure! I'm here and he obviously would rather work longer hours than spend time with me. If I still had feelings, I'd be crushed. :-) Now, I just think it's rather funny and just typical for him.

I spent the day yesterday trying to find furniture stores that deliver to the new home at a reasonable cost. My most pressing need is a place to sleep, but Steve still refuses to help in any way with using his truck to move things to the house. One store charges $130, which is way too expensive. If Steve would help, it would make things so much easier. He just drags his feet when it comes to helping me. I know he's tired, but he can always find time to do the things he wants to do and go the places he wants to go. He hasn't even offered to lift one thing into the car for me.

I've mentioned before that I am also tired; tired of a life that's gray and cold, and therefore am looking forward to a time of peace, of taking time to do oil paintings again, and to complete my latest book. I also hope to decorate the house with antiques and old, interesting pieces from yard sales and thrift shops. The house was built in 1890, so I'm trying to decorate for that period. It'll be a challenge, but fun.

I seriously doubt Steve will even visit once I'm in the new house. Again, it'd be nice if he did, but if he doesn't, it really doesn't matter anymore.

Have a nice weekend, everyone! Here in the U.S., we are celebrating Labor Day on Monday.

Escape from AS Island

Well, I made it! It's been a very busy week as you can imagine.

Before I do anything else, I want to thank you for your patience in waiting for an update, and for your encouragement. If it were possible, I'd invite you all to come and share my little house with me. It could be one big sleepover where we could support one another, telling of our AS joys, sorrows, trials and tribulations and gain the strength to go on in spite of them.

Ladies, I must tell you that I accomplished the nearly impossible this week. I ordered furniture, but the delivery charge was so high, I ended up renting a truck on my own and driving it to the place, picked up the furniture, and unloaded it all by myself. All that with a bad back, fibromyalgia, and a just healed rotator cuff injury. Sometimes you have no choice, but to do or die. I felt that if God didn't send me someone to help, He would then give me the strength to do it on my own, which He did.

I'm not talking little puny furniture, but a huge, queen-size mattress and foundation, a super heavy sleigh bed and rails, and two rocker/recliners. I have huge bruises and several little ones from my chest down, but have the satisfaction of saying "I did it!" All the while I was thinking that if Steve ever did come to the house, he'd be sleeping on the floor as I had to the first couple of nights. As my husband, he should have been there to help, but instead, he has done nothing to help with the move. Ughhh.

Steve and I talk every evening, but he still is dragging his feet about coming here. He asks whether or not I can get videos with my computer connection, which is a factor, I guess, in his making the trip. If he isn't getting his truck worked on this weekend (his major excuse for not coming), I'm going to tell him to not even bother, and I'll just stay away longer.

I must stop here after I say welcome to the new members. Thank you so much for joining us and I do hope you'll stick around and contribute to the conversations.

More about the move within the next day or two...

September 15, 2011

Our membership is growing and I realized that we are just a small representation of those who are involved in a relationship with an Aspie. There have got to be thousands more just like us!

Once someone finally realizes that AS is the reason for their mate's behavior, they usually begin to search for as much information as they can find about it. I know I did. If you have any links that you feel would help, please add them here. When I have more time, I will add them to the links section of this website. *Knowledge is power* as the saying goes.

Steve calls every evening and after a week finally said he missed me. I asked if he missed my cooking and he said, "Kinda..." He's been eating fast foods and frozen pizzas for dinner. If he doesn't miss my cooking all that much (and I'm a pretty good cook if I may say so myself), he can eat fast foods should I ever decide to go back. ☺

He still uses the excuse of having to get his truck fixed before he can come to see the house. Not true. It's taking him to work and back and everywhere else he needs to go. He just doesn't want to make the trip because it concerns something that involves me and not necessarily him. He may also be afraid of having to move things up here for me. Who knows?

I began to make a list of how our marriage has gone downhill through the years, and the things Steve used to do for me to show his love when we first got married and what he does now, which is pretty much zilch. I do not like being taken for granted. Nobody does. I've always tried to be a good wife to Steve, but get little in the way of respect in return. It's not a good place to be. Guess that's why I'm here and he's there. A wife gets tired of living that way. Eventually, after being on life support for so long, you flat line and that's about where I am now. No feelings left and no desire to try anymore.

Steve did ask when I'm coming home, but I told him there's plenty of work to do at the house and enough to keep me busy for a few more weeks. There's really no reason to return, anyway. I wish he'd give me at least one, but he couldn't if I asked him. He'd probably say something like, "Because you're my wife." That's supposed to be enough.

People in my neighborhood are wondering why they haven't seen my husband and keep asking when he's coming up here. I have to keep giving excuses, such as he's working a lot of overtime. Eventually, they may just decide that we're separated or divorced or that he's just a figment of my imagination.

Imagine a husband not even being interested in a major purchase that his wife made like a house! I tried to include him in the process, but he showed no interest. What more could I do? He wants to remain in his own little familiar world. Stepping out of his comfort zone would be more than he could handle, I guess.

I've tried to think how I would react if Steve said he was going to go out and buy a house. I know I'd be interested in seeing it and offering to help him in any way I could. If that was his dream, I'd be supportive. Wish he'd do the same for me, but that hasn't happened.

Well, enough about that.

It turned cold overnight with temps in the thirties and me with only a space heater to keep out the chill. Even with the bitter cold, it's warmer here than with Steve. I can actually see the big, blue sky and am surrounded by tall pine trees, beautiful thick shrubs, lush grass, and friendly neighbors.

Even though I'm basically on my own with little human contact, God has shown He's with me. I'm so thankful for His working out a plan where I can escape occasionally to this house, which is a place of refuge for me. I wish others in the same AS situation as I am could do the same, but I realize it's not financially possible for everybody. I am on a very limited budget, believe me, but in the area where I purchased the house, prices have hit rock bottom, so I got the house at an excellent price. I also had money set aside from the sale of property I had before Steve and I married. That is how I was able to buy the house.

The bottom dropped out in another area of my life, and I've been having to deal with that, too. It cut me to the heart, but I've learned to just go with the flow and allow God to work it out for good eventually.

The day before the closing on the house, my daughter announced that she and her family were moving 50 miles farther away. One of the reasons for choosing to buy a house in the area where they lived was so I could spend more time with my grandchildren. Instead, they are making it even more difficult. I understand their reasons for putting their house up for sale as they have a long commute to take their children to school, but it came as a complete surprise to me. The timing couldn't have been worse.

My daughter has yet to see the inside of the house and has not even offered to help me move in. She's normally quite considerate, so it was out of character for her.

Anyway, I just accept things as they are and am now just trying to do what I have to do for myself and what makes me happy. Again, it seems I'll only be able to see my grandkids the usual once or twice a year and be to them the grandma that sends them gifts and cards on Birthdays and at Christmas.

That's what's going on in my world today. What's happening in yours?

Live in the sunshine...in spite of the rain.

Week 3 at My Little Hideaway – September 21, 2011

I am settling in to a routine here at my little country house. I've had time to observe nature, enjoy the breeze blowing through the trees, dry my hair in the morning sun, and smell the freshness of clean clothes straight from the clothesline. I am relaxed, working at my own pace due to physical limitations, and making headway on projects that need to be done.

The past two nights I haven't slept very well. Last night I just felt such sadness at Steve's lack of support when it comes to helping me with this house and enjoying it with me. We talk almost every night, but when for the umpteenth time he said he might come to see the house, I finally got fed up and said to him that he should just admit it that he's not <u>ever</u> coming to see it. I also asked him why, but he was silent. He could give me no answer. At least now, we're not fooling ourselves and the subject won't be brought up again, at least by me.

Sometimes I wonder why I am where I am and why Steve is where he is, then I think of conversations like we had last night and I remember. Our marriage is nothing like it was at the first. I know people settle in to a comfortable relationship once they've been together for awhile, but it should not be that they take the other for granted and at least try to make the marriage work.

I've stated before on this blog that Steve does less and less to make me even want to stay married to him. I have no idea why he does not bother to even try. Is it AS that makes him so distant and/or lazy that he does not love and cherish me as he vowed, not treat me like hired help?

Steve says he's getting by without me there, but misses me. I think he misses me doing the work around the house more than he does me.

I'm staying away another week or two, maybe longer. Here in the Midwest, the autumn colors are the most beautiful at this time of year and I want to stick around to see them in all their brilliance. Also, I have little reason to return. Life with Steve is a drudge and when I do go back, all I'll be thinking about is my next getaway in the spring when I can come back to my peaceful, little house again.

Chapter 14 – Closing Thoughts

Being married to someone with Asperger's syndrome is extremely difficult. We have had our ups and downs like every other couple, but the difference is that the highs are few and far between, and the lows are lower than low. Nothing ever changes. It is always the same as the Aspie must continue in their own humdrum routine.

Our marriage at this point in time can be compared to the machine you see attached by wires to the patient in a hospital that detects when a heart stops beating. I believe we have flat-lined.

Our relationship has no life, but we stay connected for reasons I, myself, don't quite know. At this stage in my life, it's doubtful I'll pull the plug and call it quits, but I know for a fact, when I was a younger, healthier, individual, I would not have tolerated half of the things I do now. Perhaps I've grown tired and lazy myself and just accept my fate and the fact that the situation is never going to get any better.

I've become quite cynical, not only from the life I live today, but from past experiences with relationships. I feel my marriage to an Aspie is just another bad hand life has dealt me, even though I'm very much aware that no marriage is perfect and there will always be problems. When we step out of one situation, we walk into another one that's also filled with poop, but just on different shoes.

If I could go back in time, would I marry my husband again, knowing what I know now about Asperger's? I can honestly say I would not.

It has been emotionally draining from day one, and if I wanted just a roommate I could have moved in with a friend. It would have been easier.

When I got married, I expected to be joined to a husband in every sense of the word. I wanted a relationship filled with mutual love and respect, and romance. Someone who is capable of understanding my emotions and can read my actions, someone who would look out for me and lovingly protect me.

I wanted someone with whom I could share every aspect of my life and with whom I could grow old. I did not expect to be so alone.

A marriage should not be that way and ours falls so very far short from the ideal.

A husband should be able to comfort his wife when she needs it, but my Aspie husband just stares at me on the rare occasions I cry when I'm sad. He would never know to put his arms around me and hold me close. If I have to ask him to do that, it defeats the purpose. Mechanical comfort is no comfort at all.

A healthy marriage should involve both "give and take" but in an NT/AS relationship, it is mostly "give" on the part of the NT and "take" on the part of the Aspie.

I do love my husband, but not in the same way as I did early on. It has become like the love I have for a brother, not a spouse. I care for him and want what's best for him, but any deep feelings of married love I may have once had for him, have all died. You can't expect it to do otherwise when neglected for so long.

Because of the lack of intimacy, I would have every legal right to just walk away and leave him on his own since he seems to prefer being in his own little world anyway. It's called *abandonment* and valid grounds for divorce.

My relationship with my husband is calm and predictable. There is no violence or physical abuse, such as I experienced in my first two marriages, but there is emotional abuse whether intentional or not.

I thought for years that Steve didn't love me because of something in me that was flawed and it made me feel terrible. I cried often over what I thought were intentional slights and a lack of sensitivity to my needs. I've gotten past all that and have learned to suppress any such feelings.

Oh, if I had only known it was AS at the start, many things would have been easier and my health and psyche wouldn't have suffered so long and so often.

People need to know what AS is and how to spot it. It can aid Aspies in getting an earlier diagnosis as so many only stumble upon what is wrong with them in middle age after much damage has already been done. Counseling and medication should be recommended so as to improve their quality of life.

Steve continues to remain in denial about his having Asperger's, so will never submit to medication or counseling to help him control it. He chooses to ignore anything that might interfere with the little cocoon of a life he's created for himself. He is comfortable there and that's all that matters to him. If he would step outside of himself just for a time to get help, I believe it would relieve a lot of stress and anxiety for both of us.   I pray that may happen one day, but it would take a miracle.

*   *   *

If, after reading my story, you still choose to enter into a relationship with an Aspie, it is your choice. It may be like running straight into a house you know is on fire, but again, it's your decision.

Whatever you decide, I wish you the best and ask that you get involved with Asperger's awareness by recommending this book to your friends.

Sincerely,

Asperger Wife

Made in the USA
Middletown, DE
24 November 2014